The
Healthy
Workplace

Leigh Stringer, LEED AP

The Healthy Workplace

How to Improve the Well-Being of
Your Employees—and Boost Your
Company's Bottom Line

AMERICAN MANAGEMENT ASSOCIATION
New York • Atlanta • Brussels • Chicago • Mexico City • San Francisco
Shanghai • Tokyo • Toronto • Washington, D.C.

Bulk discounts available. For details visit:
www.amacombooks.org/go/specialsales
Or contact special sales:
Phone: 800-250-5308
E-mail: specialsls@amanet.org
View all the AMACOM titles at: www.amacombooks.org
American Management Association: www.amanet.org

This publication is designed to provide accurate and authoritative information in regard to the subject matter covered. It is sold with the understanding that the publisher is not engaged in rendering legal, accounting, or other professional service. If legal advice or other expert assistance is required, the services of a competent professional person should be sought.

Library of Congress Cataloging-in-Publication Data

Names: Stringer, Leigh, author.
Title: The healthy workplace : how to improve the well-being of your
  employees–and boost your company's bottom line / Leigh Stringer.
Description: New York : American Management Association, [2016] | Includes
  bibliographical references and index.
Identifiers: LCCN 2015051076 (print) | LCCN 2016005865 (ebook) | ISBN
  9780814437438 (hardcover) | ISBN 9780814437445 (ebook)
Subjects: LCSH: Employee health promotion. | Industrial hygiene. | Corporate
  culture.
Classification: LCC RC969.H43 S77 2016 (print) | LCC RC969.H43 (ebook) | DDC
  362.1068/3–dc23
LC record available at http://lccn.loc.gov/2015051076

About AMA
American Management Association (www.amanet.org) is a world leader in talent development, advancing the skills of individuals to drive business success. Our mission is to support the goals of individuals and organizations through a complete range of products and services, including classroom and virtual seminars, webcasts, webinars, podcasts, conferences, corporate and government solutions, business books, and research. AMA's approach to improving performance combines experiential learning—learning through doing—with opportunities for ongoing professional growth at every step of one's career journey.

Printing number

10 9 8 7 6 5 4 3 2 1

To Kate and Ali

CONTENTS

Preface

"I realize it has become too easy to find a diet to fit in with whatever you happen to feel like eating and that diets are not there to be picked and mixed but picked and stuck to, which is exactly what I shall begin to do once I've eaten this chocolate croissant."

—Helen Fielding, *Bridget Jones's Diary*

"DOES THIS CHAIR MAKE MY butt look fat?" After laughing, my husband, John, got a worried look and stopped in his tracks. "Uh, are you serious?" he asked. I realized, of course, that no man in his right mind would dare answer this question, but I really wanted to know. "I'm not saying you need to answer me, but honestly, I spend all day at work sitting at my desk and staring at a computer. I feel like I've been working this way for ages and that it's finally catching up with me. Do you think being chained to a chair has something to do with my midsection spread?" John agreed—very carefully—that yes, he felt that his job, similarly involving staring at a computer for many hours, was not exactly benefiting his health, and slow weight gain and stress were bothering him, too. Up until recently, we had both regularly complained that we did not get enough time to work out and we continually felt frustrated and guilty about it. At least in my case, I was surprised—almost shocked—by how my health was deteriorating. I mean, I thought I was doing everything right. But the truth was that I had been neglecting my body and avoiding the stress toll of work for years, and it was finally time to do something about it.

To give a little history, I have spent the last 25 years of my life being a very hard worker. From the time I graduated from high school to today, I have been employed by eight different companies in six different cities and two countries. When the company I worked for needed me to move, I moved. When I needed to cancel my vacation because of a big project, I canceled it. When my boss or my team needed me to work overtime, I did it. Then I had two beautiful girls. But I kept going because I really love working and the pride I feel having accomplished something at the end of the day. I want my girls to know that women can do anything they set their minds to and that being a mother and having a career is totally possible. I wrote my first book, *The Green Workplace*, with my first daughter—two years old at the time—swinging from my legs. I moved to New York City when my second daughter was still a newborn to build up my firm's consulting practice there. I was awarded the "top 40 under 40" award for professionals in the building industry, was one of the youngest people appointed to my company's board of directors at the time, and became a senior vice president at what most would consider an early age. I have had some of the best clients on the planet and am considered one of the world's leading workplace design experts. I attribute this success to an amazingly supportive family, brilliant and inspiring colleagues, great mentors, but also to really, really hard work.

I guess you could say things were going pretty well for me career-wise. Then, almost out of nowhere, I just hit a wall. After several months of supporting an important client on a major project, I became physically and mentally drained and had no energy for work, family, or friends. The months and months of overtime and the years of bad health habits had caught up with me. My mood was terrible: I was snappy, lethargic, and tuned out. I was drinking large amounts of coffee during the day and then compensating with a glass or two of wine at night to settle down. I was eating cupcakes, chocolate, and snacks around the office and at home and ordering takeout pretty regularly. I was not really exercising, and when I did, it would really mess up my day and get in the way of other more important tasks, like work or taking care of my kids. At one point in my life, I actually ran a marathon, but that was years ago. At this point, I could barely run two miles without feeling as if I would pass out. Health just was not a priority.

I was the queen of excuses when it came to weight gain. At one point, I added up all the reasons I had put on pounds. The list reads a bit like an entry in *Bridget Jones's Diary*.

LEGITIMATE EXCUSES FOR WEIGHT GAIN

- *Over 40 years old, add 5 pounds.* I was over 40, so that meant I was "supposed" to add on 5 more pounds. I mean, at 40 your metabolism slows down and there is not much you can do about that.
- *Giving birth to two children, add 5 pounds each.* Having two children clearly gave me a free pass for going up at least a dress size. Again, body changes happen when you are pregnant and afterward, and other people gain weight because of having kids, so I have to be fair to myself.
- *Working in a stressful industry, add 10 pounds.* I work for a design firm and architects are *supposed* to work really hard and throw everything into their work. It's the culture of our industry! In college, we used to brag about how many all-nighters we pulled in a row. In most of the design firms I have worked for, there has been an unspoken rule that "hours put in" are required for advancement.
- *Working in the modern age, add 5 pounds.* Even if I am not at the office, I am expected to respond to emails at all hours of the day. Hey, the world is global and 24/7. It's just how work is today. So shouldn't I get a few bonus pounds because I'm just being a good employee and sacrificing health for my trade?

Even as I write these excuses down, they sound ridiculous. But the truth is that I was overweight, in bad health, and in denial about it.

And the worst part was that clothes didn't hide it anymore. Now I am a fairly confident person and do not tend to obsess over appearance, but there was a point when I called in to a videoconference from my laptop and was shocked at my own image. My face was swollen and broken out, and no matter how subtly I tried to turn my head in a way that was flattering, my face just looked like a red blotchy balloon—kind of like the face of Vernon Dursley, Harry Potter's uncle, in the movies. There was just no "good side" (no offense to Richard Griffiths, the actor who played Uncle Vernon). And then there was the time on the New York City subway when a guy got up to give me his seat. Normally, I would be pleasantly surprised by this (I mean, I can count on two hands the times I have seen this kind of chivalry happen on the New York subway), only he was getting up because he thought I was pregnant. Of course, at certain points in my life this would have been a very appropriate thing, but when this happened, my youngest child was almost three years old. At first I thought this was a fluke until it happened several more times. After about the third time, I just got snappy. "You can just keep your seat, thank you very much. I don't need it! I'm not pregnant and I'm not *old*!"

During the really stressful project I mentioned earlier, when I hit that wall, I realized I needed to seriously challenge some assumptions I had about my definition for success. I mean, my career looked good on paper, but I was losing interest and drive and my health was not in a good place. Plus, there were times when I found myself yelling at my children for things that were just plain not their fault. At one point, during an 8 p.m. conference call, I chased my eight-year-old out of her room because it was the quietest place in the house and I needed to get work done. She was tired and it was her bedtime, but work comes first, right? And then there was the time I took my girls to the office with me because my husband was feeling like a single parent and was tired of doing all of the kid duties at night (mostly because I was so busy working at home). So I dragged the girls to the office at 6 p.m. and got home three hours later. I know, bad choice. Let us just say no one was particularly happy that evening.

I think the tipping point for me was one Friday night at 11:30 p.m. when I got an angry email from a client. I probably should not have been checking my email at that time, and my client probably should not have sent the email, because it prevented us both from sleeping well. The next day, I sat at my desk in tears thinking, "I hate you Sheryl Sandberg . . . leaning in just sucks."[1] I just felt so frustrated that my life was so out of balance and so unhealthy and that I could not make anyone happy, not even the client I was busting my butt to support. After several long talks with my husband, who gradually talked me off the ledge, I began to imagine a different life for myself. I had been working so hard for so long that this was actually pretty difficult to do. Plus, everyone around me seemed to think I was perfectly fine. One of my colleagues whom I hadn't seen in years came up to me and in a burst of generosity said, "You know, you really are living the dream!" But if this was the dream—working like a crazy person and operating on fumes all the time—then I did not want it anymore. I have spent my entire life thinking that hard work would lead to good things, and it just was not working for me any longer. It was at this time that I decided to stop working so hard and start working *smart*.

Over the years, I have spoken to a range of health experts who all consistently stress how important it is to perform moderate exercise for at least 2½ hours a week in order to stay healthy and minimize weight gain. They are just following guidelines put forth by the U.S. Department of Health and Human Services, the World Health Organization, and other notable agencies.[2] But in the past, the more I heard this advice, the more upset I would get. I mean, "working out" is more than just working out. It requires driving to the gym, changing clothes, working up a sweat, cooling down, showering, drying hair, and applying makeup (for some of us). By my count, that 2½ hours easily grows to 10 or 12 hours a week, depending on how often and how long your workout lasts. And how is it possible to squeeze working out in between waking up, getting breakfast ready, making lunches, getting the children to and from school, commuting to and from work, working nine hours, making dinner, doing homework, and getting everyone to bed? How about just a little time to myself? I find it exceptionally difficult to take a yoga class or head to the gym most weeks, and when I do, I feel like I am taking time away from something else I am supposed to be doing. Well, apparently, I am not alone. Only one in 20 Americans actually meets nationally recommended exercise goals.[3]

Of course, the ironic thing is that I love exercise and moving around. I get great ideas and have tremendous energy when I walk, run, spin, hike, and do yoga, and I would love nothing more than to keep that feeling all day. In fact, there is mounting evidence that exercise, movement, and relaxing the brain in general are excellent ways to spawn innovative new ideas.[4] But there is only so much time available when I am working 40 to 60 hours a week. I mean, something had to give! And then it hit me. What if I fundamentally changed the way I work in such a way that it helps me lose weight, reduce stress, and increase productivity *during the workday*? What if I were to change my workplace so it enables (instead of hinders) healthy habits?

It is worth mentioning that this book started out as a self-help book. I swore that if the research for this book helped just one person—me—it would still be worth all the effort! But after some due diligence, I found that vast numbers of people like me are already trying hard to be healthy at work, as measured by lots of anecdotal evidence but also by our spending habits. The health and wellness industry is exploding and estimated to top $1 trillion by 2017.[5] Most workers really want to be healthy. The message about the importance of being healthy at work—at least for individuals—is not new at all. But there is a gap in the marketplace when it comes to helping employers keep their workers engaged, healthy, and productive. Most companies today are fairly reactive when it comes to employee health, offering insurance or counseling to save on insurance costs, but they do not take a proactive role in improving the health of their workforce. So, at the advice of many, the focus of this book took a turn, and I started to investigate ways to not only help employees but also ways to help employers better support and improve the performance of a workforce that is desperate for their help.

I know a great deal about the workplace and how it can be used as a force for good from my practice and research on the topic over the last couple of decades, but most of my work has been focused on work from a space perspective: how people use space and adapt it to better suit their needs, how space can be a catalyst to change behaviors at work, and the physical aspects of a healthy work environment. But to really dig into the topic, I needed to better understand all facets of health as they relate to work and the workplace, including nutrition, movement, mental health, and sleep. So I jumped in with both feet, Tim Ferriss–style, using myself as a research tool, trying on new fitness techniques, eating different foods, and taking on new, healthy behaviors.[6] I visited Miraval, a state-of-the-art health and wellness center in Tucson, Arizona. I participated in the Corporate Athlete® program in Orlando, Florida, at the Johnson & Johnson Human Performance Institute, where I was analyzed physically from head to toe and learned how elite athletes manage and maintain their energy and performance, and how this applies to the rest of us. I attended a conference in New York called Wisdom 2.0 Business about mindfulness in the workplace and stress reduction techniques that progressive business leaders are using to keep their cool and focus. And I talked to a lot of people.

I think it's fair to say that in researching this book, I became completely obsessed with the topic of engagement, health, wellness, and human performance. I interviewed paleoanthropologists, environmental psychologists, educators, sports coaches, medical professionals, nutritionists, sleep specialists, ergonomists, exercise physiologists, and companies on the leading edge of providing health and wellness programs for their employees. I began working with the Harvard School of Public Health on a new Health and Human Performance Index that measures health, engagement, and a healthy work environment—and the impact of these factors on the bottom line. I also joined in with the Center for Active Design in New York to create Workplace Wellness Guidelines, which will provide a new standard for how the physical environment can support health and performance when it comes to work. As a companion to my research and to the book content, I created a Facebook page (www.Facebook.com/TheHealthyWorkplaceBook) and a blog (LeighStringer.com)where I continue to post tips and health-related articles daily. It taught me what people were really starving to hear about and what they felt worthy of sharing.

With the lessons and case studies from this book, employers and employees will be empowered to make the simple changes necessary to turn their workplaces from a *drain* on employee health and engagement to a *contributor* to it.

HOW TO READ THIS BOOK

The first few chapters of the book explore some of the health issues out there caused by work and why work is the place to help solve them. It takes a step back and looks at our distant past, digging into how early humans have lived over the last several thousand years and how the relationship between work and human health has changed. It dissects productivity and performance from a business perspective and discusses ways to maximize this by tapping into flow, group flow, and the more creative parts of our brain.

Then, starting in Chapter 4 and continuing through Chapter 7, it takes a deeper look at the human engine itself, to better understand how it can be calibrated to its maximum efficiency and effectiveness at work. In order to do this, it challenges the current paradigms at work today that shape the way we move, eat, handle stress, sit . . . even how we sleep. More importantly, it identifies specific strategies that research validates and leading-edge companies have tested; hopefully, they will work for your organization, your team, or even you as an individual.

The last two chapters in the book put all of the elements of a healthy workplace together. Chapter 8 tells the stories of companies that have integrated many of the strategies listed in the book and embody a culture of health, which has impacted their bottom line. It also lays out some of the more effective ways to change employee behavior. Chapter 9, the last chapter, helps you build a business case and create a roadmap for improving the individual performance of employees in your organization. It also gives a couple of different views into the future. And finally, there is a checklist of healthy strategies in the Afterword.

I encourage you to skip around. Don't feel like you have to be a purist and read this book from start to finish. I promise, I won't be offended! Honestly, the last thing I want to do is to add more stress to your life. Try reading a chapter that has the most interest for you personally or start with an area where you think your organization could use the most help. If your organization has already addressed some of the ideas described here, fantastic; just move on to the next section. And if you read this book all the way through and find yourself hungry for more, try reading some of my favorite books about all things health, well-being, and productivity listed in Suggested Reading at the end.

I wish you well on your journey to health.

Leigh Stringer
October 2015
Washington, DC

The
Healthy
Workplace

Health and the "Bottom" Line

I T WAS A HOT DAY in Orlando, Florida, and I was in my swimsuit. But instead of lounging by the pool, I was sitting, somewhat self-consciously, in an instrument called the BOD POD®. This large, white, egg-shaped machine bears a strong resemblance to Robin Williams's spaceship in the sitcom *Mork & Mindy*. The physiologist operating the machine asked me to sit as still as possible and breathe normally, which was a little difficult to do because I'm slightly claustrophobic and the egg didn't have a lot of wiggle room on the inside. But sitting still, I learned later, was important for the machine to work. As I sat there quietly, nervously chanting to myself, "Mork calling Orson, come in Orson," to keep from having a panic attack, the BOD POD® was hard at work. This machine, one of the most specialized of its kind, uses air displacement plethysmography technology and is designed to measure body composition.[1] Specifically, it tallies body fat and lean mass and gives accurate estimates of the amount of kilocalories burned daily at a resting metabolic rate and at varying levels (sedentary, low activity, active, or high activity).[2] For trainers who use the device with elite athletes, this is a highly useful tool for helping their clients fuel themselves appropriately, matching calories consumed to calories burned, which typically varies during the course of the day based on their workout schedule.

At the Johnson & Johnson Human Performance Institute (JJHPI) in Orlando, where I was that day, the BOD POD® was being used on a group of corporate executives from all over the world as one of the first activities for their Corporate Athlete course. Technicians were measuring our baseline data, with information from the BOD POD® and a blood draw, to provide all of the participants in the course with a snapshot of their health. JJHPI does this so that participants in the course face the truth about their current physical health situation. For many of us, the detailed information we received about our glucose levels, cholesterol, and vitamin deficiencies was not unexpected. For some of us, though, this information was a bit of a shock, and I was one of those people. My numbers said that I was no longer the Sporty Spice long-distance power runner I was 10 years ago. Instead, I was solidly in the category of having too much excess fat, and I was clearly overweight. Ouch. And so, with a jolt, began my reeducation about health, wellness, and the need to make necessary changes at work, at home, and in all aspects of my life. [3]

I first learned about JJHPI from some of my corporate clients. This Corporate Athlete® course is a program they raved about, and it specifically caters to corporate executives, not elite athletes (though JJHPI trains them too). The Corporate Athlete® program has included employees from Glaxo-SmithKline (GSK), Deere & Company, Pepsico, Estee Lauder, Morgan Stanley, Allstate, and Johnson & Johnson (J&J) on a regular basis. In fact, J&J has sent more than 50,000 employees through the course to date (in several formats) and aims to train many more employees globally as part of its overall health and wellness program. J&J leaders believe in it so much that they bought the company.

2

JJHPI was cofounded in 1991 by Dr. Jim Loehr, a performance psychologist, and Dr. Jack Groppel, an authority on human performance, fitness, and nutrition. One of Loehr and Groppel's early research findings came from training professional athletes—clients like tennis pros Jim Courier, Monica Seles, and Pete Sampras, golfer Mark O'Meara, Pro Bowl quarterback Jim Harbaugh, hockey players Eric Lindros and Mike Richter, Indy 500 champion Eddie Cheever, Jr., and Olympic gold medal speedskater Dan Jansen. It's an impressive list.

Over time, Loehr and Groppel found that all of the athletes they trained were excellent technically, but the difference between the good and the great players was their ability to manage energy, both in their training and during competitions. Loehr and Groppel started studying energy management at the cellular level, which led them to develop a comprehensive science-based program for exercise, nutrition intake, sleep, and other forms of recovery throughout the day. They also developed a unique, multidimensional (physical, emotional, mental, and spiritual) behavior change model. Athletes, and also the rest of us, need to be high functioning on many levels to give our best performance on the field or in our jobs. And our behaviors on a daily basis can really inhibit or enable our performance. The Corporate Athlete® program focuses in on what those behaviors are and how to modify them.

It is fair to say that the companies sending their senior leaders to the Corporate Athlete® course are seeing a lack of energy and engagement in their employees and in general, and they clearly believe that paying for leaders to attend training is a worthwhile investment, not just in the lives of their people but in the value of their company. Several studies conducted to evaluate the Corporate Athlete® course suggest JJHPI is on to something pretty powerful. When surveyed, graduates of the course suggested they had more energy, better mental health, better emotional well-being, and better general health, even 18 months after they took the course.[4] When course-takers were

3

asked to rate their performance over that time, they said they improved productivity based on worktime missed, time spent actually working, and "the extent to which health is affecting both work productivity and regular daily activities."[5] Considering that most of the people taking the course are generally pretty healthy to start, it's impressive to see these positive changes.

A study performed by GlaxoSmithKline assessed how the Corporate Athlete® training impacted companies at the organizational level. It evaluated the relationship between Corporate Athlete® training and changes in on-the-job behavior, comparing leaders who had taken the course to their peers. Program graduates achieved more favorable assessment ratings on all behaviors, most notably on their "developing people" behavior. Results suggest that investing in leaders in this way may foster a culture of employee empowerment.[6] We'll touch more on the Corporate Athlete® course and some of their specific strategies in Chapter 4 and Chapter 8.

I'LL HAVE WHAT SHE'S HAVING

Leading companies like Google, Facebook, Apple, Next Jump, Under Armour, Aetna, The Motley Fool, Owens Corning, and Johnson & Johnson have learned that to stay ahead and compete, they have to take the health of their employees more seriously than they might have in the past, not just to save costs but also to acquire new talent and take full advantage of the talent they already employ. Healthy employees are more creative, productive, and engaged and are less prone to take sick days and suffer from chronic illnesses. Employees are the engine that keeps companies running. And healthy employees, who are emotionally, mentally, and physically prepared to take on whatever challenge is in front of them, are more likely to make the companies they work for grow and flourish.

Seems pretty simple, right? So why are most workplaces so

unhealthy? Did we just fall asleep at the wheel? It turns out that in a way that is true. Without our paying attention, the way we work has changed and our work style is such that our workplaces are no longer supporting our health or productivity. Over the last 50 years, especially, we have become more and more sedentary, staring at electronic devices for long periods of time with very few breaks. And when those breaks are taken, it's typically for a fast-food lunch or a sugary snack from a nearby vending machine. As a result, 70 percent of Americans are overweight (and suffering from a host of diseases associated with it, many potentially fatal), along with having chronic physical ailments including neck, back, and shoulder pain, headaches, and eyestrain. Since work no longer ends when the traditional 9 to 5 workday does, workers suffer from a lack of exercise and sleep, poor nutrition, and stress. And the physical environment they occupy is not exactly helping either. Most workers struggle with poor ergonomics, air quality, lighting, and views to the outdoors, as well as problems with thermal comfort and acoustics. Taken together, all these factors combine to make the hours spent in the workplace the least healthy part of the day.

THE PROBLEMS WE HAVE TO SOLVE

You cannot watch the news today in America without hearing about the cost of health care. In 2013, the United States spent more than $2.9 trillion annually, or 17.4 percent of the gross domestic product, on health care services, more than any other country.[7] A large majority of the cost goes to treating noncommunicable, chronic illnesses like diabetes, heart disease, lung disease, and Alzheimer's. Chronic diseases cause 7 out of 10 deaths and account for 80 percent of dollars spent on health care in the United States.[8] And the rise in such diseases is a quickly growing problem that is contributing to rising health care costs. In 2012, U.S. employers spent \$578.6 billion on group health care coverage, which is a 72 percent increase over the \$336.1 billion spent in 2000.[9] In addition, a global survey of business executives conducted by the World Economic Forum and the Harvard School of Public Health from 2009 to 2011 identified noncommunicable diseases as one of the leading threats to global economic growth.[10]

Let's look at some of the specific health problems facing us today.

■ Obesity

One of the contributors to many of these chronic diseases is being overweight and in particular being obese, now reaching epidemic proportions. Obesity levels in American adults doubled from 1980 to 2012.[11] The problem does not just exist in the United States. Across the countries in the Organization for Economic Co-operation and Development (OECD), 18 percent of the adult population is obese. More than one in three adults in Mexico, New Zealand, and the United States, and more than one in four in Australia, Canada, Chile, and Hungary, are obese.[12] In the United States, obese men incur \$1152 more in direct annual health costs than normal-weight men, and obese women incur \$3613 more than normal-weight women.[13] Overweight men miss 56 percent more days of work per year than normal-weight men, and overweight women miss 15 percent more days than normal-weight women.[14]

Research shows that as people become overweight and obese, their risk for developing a number of chronic diseases goes up, including coronary heart disease, type 2 diabetes, various cancers (endometrial, breast, and colon), hypertension (or high blood pressure), dyslipidemia (for example, high total cholesterol or high levels of triglycerides), stroke, liver and gallbladder disease, sleep apnea and breathing problems, osteoarthritis (a breakdown of cartilage and bone within a joint), and gynecological problems (such as abnormal periods and infertility).[15] This is truly a frightening list.

▪ Smoking

Worldwide, tobacco use causes nearly 6 million deaths per year, and current trends show that tobacco use will cause more than 8 million deaths annually by 2030.[16] Even though smoking does not happen inside workplaces (in most industrialized countries, anyway), there are still millions of people racing to the front doors of buildings everywhere to smoke several times a day. According to the Centers for Disease Control, tobacco use remains the leading cause of preventable morbidity and mortality in the United States.[17]

▪ Musculoskeletal Issues

Pain in our bodies plagues us and is perpetuated by our work. Musculoskeletal disorders (MSDs) and diseases are the leading cause of disability in the United States and account for more than half of all chronic conditions in people over 50 years of age in developed countries. The annual direct and indirect costs for bone and joint health in the United States are $950 billion, roughly 7.4 percent of the U.S. gross domestic product.[18] In the UK, the total number of working days lost due to MSDs in 2013–2014 was 8.3 million, an average of 15.9 days per case of MSDs (out of 526,000 cases that year).[19]

Even if you do not engage in heavy labor, the act of repetitive motion or even lack of motion for long periods can still cause all sorts of problems. Our sedentary behavior is also putting us at risk for cardio metabolic risk factors like diabetes, heart disease, and stroke, and they are causing an increase in the number of cases of deep vein thrombosis (blood clots in the legs), which has been traditionally associated with heavy travel but also is regularly caused by long periods of sitting.[20]

■ Stress

Another major contributor to our health issues is workplace stress. Not all stress is bad, but stress overload can negatively affect our mental and physical health, decrease productivity, and lead to burnout. According to a recent survey from the American Psychological Association, 42 percent of adults report that their stress level has increased (36 percent say their stress level has stayed the same) over the past five years. Stress can negatively impact sleep, eating patterns, and our willingness to exercise.[21] It is often caused by changing job requirements, the lack of involvement in decision making, lack of recognition, poor working relationships, poor physical working conditions, or long or erratic work schedules. The World Health Organization estimates that stress costs American businesses $300 billion a year. And that does not include the negative impact on our personal lives.

■ Absenteeism and Presenteeism

All this chronic illness has caused increases in absenteeism and presenteeism (which is going to work while being sick or not fully engaged). Walter Stewart, a director of the Center for Health Research and Rural Advocacy at Geisinger Health System in Danville, Pennsylvania, engaged in a yearlong survey of roughly 29,000 working American adults. He calculated the total cost of presenteeism in the United States to be more than $150 billion per year.[22] Another study from the *Journal of Occupational and Environmental Medicine* found that the on-the-job productivity loss resulting from depression/anxiety, obesity, arthritis, and back/neck pain was 2.3 times greater than the absence-related productivity loss attributed to these conditions.[23] In other words, less time was actually lost from people staying home than from people showing up to work not fully charged.

Human resources groups are scrambling to evaluate company contributions to health insurance premiums for their employees and searching for impactful ways to increase wellness through preventive care, health screening, education, organized activities, incentives, and rewards. But is this really enough? Are we just trying to slap Band-Aids on a chronic health problem, or should we be trying to eliminate these problems in the first place? And can we literally change the way we work—integrate movement, improve our diet, and engage in relaxation techniques—so that we lose weight, reduce stress, increase our productivity, and prevent these chronic diseases and ailments before they even start?

LET'S RETHINK THE WORKDAY

It turns out that despite what some pharmaceutical companies would like us to think, there is no magic pill you can take to turn into Wonder Woman or Superman. But fortunately, the basic elements of keeping us at our healthy best are pretty straightforward. They include getting enough sleep, good nutrition, integrating movement and exercise throughout the day, maintaining healthy stress levels, and working in a healthy environment. It sounds so ridiculously simple, so why is it so hard to achieve? A big reason is that what our minds and bodies need at a basic level *is in conflict* with our work style. Consider this:

- ▶ *Sleep.* Our bodies need rest, but we have artificial lighting, technology, and work expectations that wreak havoc on our natural rhythms and keep us up all hours of the night. This causes all kinds of health and productivity issues.
- ▶ *Nutrition.* We eat foods at work that have been processed to the point that our bodies do not know how to digest

them efficiently. Have you looked at what is in the vending machine at your office?

▶ *Movement.* Many workers are sitting for long hours of the day (for the average American, that includes the majority of waking hours, including time spent eating, commuting, and slumped over a desk working) and moving or exercising far less than they should.[24]

▶ *Mental Health.* We are in a continual state of stress (for many, work can be 24/7), and our brains don't get the breaks they need to refresh, reenergize, and refocus. We are typically not trained to deal with this stress, or to be mindful of how it affects our mental and physical health.

▶ *Environment.* The physical setting for work is counterproductive and often sends messages that health is not a priority. This can include issues with air quality, lighting and views, thermal comfort, ergonomics, acoustics, or just the fact that the workspace makes it difficult to move, exercise, or find a place to recover from stress during the day.

▶ *Culture and Community.* Organizational norms impact our behaviors at work. Sometimes workplace culture and community can support well-being, and sometimes they can be a barrier, such as the pressure to work long hours, to not take vacation days, to eat unhealthy foods, or to answer emails late at night.

WHY WORK IS THE RIGHT TIME AND PLACE FOR CHANGE

There are several arguments for why employers should invest in the health and engagement of their workforce. Here are three big ones.

■ Employees Spend More Time at Work
than They Do Anywhere Else

There are a limited number of hours in the day, and employees
spend more waking hours working than not. Waiting for a better time—that is, after hours—to get healthy does not make
sense, and here is why. During the typical workday, average
American workers commute 25.4 minutes each way, according
to the U.S. Census Bureau—close to an hour round-trip.[25] (It's
an average of 1 hour 50 minutes a day if you live in Shanghai,
1 hour 26 minutes for Rio de Janeiro, and 1 hour 14 minutes
for London.[26]) Then, they spend 7.5 hours working, plus another hour for lunch and breaks. And if your employees are
overachievers and work extra hours at home before or after
work or on weekends, they likely spent an additional 1.5 hours
of the workday donating some of their own time to work purposes.[27] So now your workers have spent 11 waking hours "on
the clock" from the time they leave their house to the time they
arrive back home. Assuming they sleep for 7.5 hours, that leaves
5.5 hours of a 24-hour workday to fit in everything else, like
cooking, cleaning, working out, winding down, and being there
for friends and family.

So what if you encourage employees to wait until the weekend to get in all of their exercise? Studies show that if people
wait to work out on two consecutive days a week to get the
recommended amount of exercise, they are not likely to meet
the weekly target (150 minutes).[28] It is just too much exercise
to fit into too brief a time period. Trying to fit all the exercise
into just a couple of days also increases their chances for injury. Weekend warriors—as well as do-it-yourselfers trying to
fit in major home improvements, yard work, etc., during the
weekend—regularly injure themselves by pushing themselves
too hard, too infrequently.[29] The same goes for nutrition,
stress reduction, and sleep. Waiting for the weekend won't
cut it. The bottom line is that workers need a consistent

11

health plan that keeps them strong and full of energy all day and all week.

■ Investing in Employee Health and Well-Being Has a Strong ROI

Johnson & Johnson (J&J) has approximately 126,500 employees working at one of 265 operating companies in 60 countries. J&J doesn't just think its health program is a good idea—the company believes it is good for business. To prove the theory, J&J looked at the cost and impact of its worksite health promotion program from 2002 to 2008. Company employees benefited from meaningful reductions in rates of obesity, high blood pressure, high cholesterol, tobacco use, physical inactivity, and poor nutrition. Average annual per employee savings were $565 in 2009 dollars, producing a return on investment (ROI) equal to a range of $1.88 to $3.92 saved for every dollar spent on the program. Measured against similar large companies, J&J experienced average annual growth in total medical spending that was 3.7 percentage points lower.[30]

And J&J is not an outlier. Harvard researchers Katherine Baicker, David Cutler, and Zirui Song, in a meta-analysis of the costs and savings associated with health and wellness programs, found that medical costs fall by about $3.27 for every dollar spent on wellness programs and that absenteeism costs fall by about $2.73 for every dollar spent.[31] This is an ROI of 6 to 1.

■ Engaged and Healthy Employees Increase Financial Performance

Having healthy employees doesn't just reduce overhead spending. It also bolsters business success overall. Recently, Dr. Raymond Fabius and a team of researchers published a study that looked at companies from 1997 to 2012 and also from

1999 to 2012 that had won the American College of Occupational Medicine's Corporate Health Achievement Award (CHAA). The researchers compared the performance of these companies to the Standard & Poor 500. Companies that win the CHAA are recognized for their exemplary efforts in creating a healthy workforce and culture and are graded on standards of practice that fall under the categories of leadership and management, healthy workers, healthy environment, and healthy organizations. The performance of these companies that invest more in employee health versus the S&P 500 are striking. Over the test period, CHAA companies had an annualized return for the portfolio of between 3.03 and 5.27 percent versus the S&P 500 annualized return of −0.06 percent. The CHAA portfolio outperformed the S&P in 9 of 13 annual periods included in the analysis. The researchers tried this same analysis changing the years of participation, changing the specific healthy companies in the portfolio, and other factors, all with similar results.[32]

To summarize, though the current state of our health is somewhat frightening, the good news is that leading companies and organizations are seeing immediate and long-lasting benefits from investing in the health and well-being of their employees. The most obvious benefits to the bottom line are the avoidance of health care costs, but companies that make investments in employee health are also seeing increases in creativity, engagement, and productivity, and as a result, business growth. How so? When companies pay attention to all of the elements that employees need to be fully charged and to have the energy and mental fortitude to do their job well—not just to focus on outcomes—a shift happens. Employees believe their company has their back so they feel cared for, engaged, and excited to come to work every day. Their customers notice and the community where they do business also sees the difference. This extra spring in their step and the added value that comes with it is a real competitive advantage.

Maybe, at this point, the business case and some of the anecdotes shared so far are enough to convince you to take another look at the health of your employees and the impact on your business. Or maybe you are still skeptical about the negative impact of work on health. I mean, let's put things in perspective. Worker safety standards globally at are an all-time high. We have all kinds of government organizations setting policy and health standards like the Occupational Safety and Health Administration and the Clean Air Act. We have more nutrition-packed food in many areas of the industrialized world than is even needed. Technology has taken many of the most hazardous jobs out of commission. On the whole, work itself has gotten much easier than in generations past, so why is work and the workplace such a problem? Aren't things actually on a trajectory to get better? Like some of you, I was a little puzzled by this paradox. Life has never been better, yet we are suffering. It turns out that getting to the bottom of this required some digging into our distant past.

2

The Evolution of Work

T HE NATIONAL MUSEUM OF NATURAL History in DC ranks as one of my favorite Smithsonian institutions of all time. If you get the chance, visit the Hall of Human Origins, put together by some of the most renowned scientists and researchers on the history of human fossils and artifacts in the world. The exhibit is organized as a chronological story of human history with displays of skulls, animal bones, cave paintings, and other archeological discoveries. The researchers who designed the exhibit cleverly explain how our bodies, brains, and behavior evolved over several million years and how this shaped how we live and look today. Probably the most impactful part of the exhibit for me was walking by the artistically rendered life-size busts of early humans. I remember reading about many of these early hominids in college, like *Australopithecus afarensis* (Lucy), *Homo erectus* (Walking Man), and *Homo neanderthalensis* (Neanderthals), and this exhibit really made them feel more real.[1]

Walking through time in this way got me thinking more deeply about our past and the major milestones that have transformed how we live and work today. According to the exhibit's timeline, 6 million years ago we began walking upright, 2.6 million years ago we started eating meat, 1.8 million years ago we started traveling (using our long legs to move from Africa all across the Earth), 800,000 years ago we began cooking, and only 10,500 years ago we started farming and domesticating animals. But the most striking evolution, from a food and exercise point of view, happened sometime between 1 million and 800,000 years ago to our evolutionary grandparents, *H. erectus.*

WALKING MAN

Early humans ate mostly plants, roots, and bark—a similar diet to chimpanzees, gorillas, and other primates today. But starting with *H. erectus*, anthropological evidence shows a major change in brain size, body size, diet composition, and foraging behavior that had a profound influence and shaped our nutritional and energy demands forever more.[2] During this time, our brain size started outpacing our body size (proportionately) so much so that if you look at human skulls before and after this time, we almost appear to be a totally different species. Most scientists believe our brain enlargement (and the shortening of our intestines) was the result of an increase in the quality of nutrition in our diet (meat, bone marrow, and other nutritionally dense foods), and some believe it coincided with the invention of cooking, when we figured out how to extract more nutrients out of what we ate.[3]

This nutrition density in our diet caused our brains to grow, so much so that the human brain beginning then, and still today, consumes roughly 20 percent of the calories we take in each day. To feed our hungry heads, we had to search for more and more nutrients, which incentivized us to look for even more kinds of nutrient-rich foods.[4] With all this motivation to expand our palate, I cannot help but think about my steely resolve to push my kids to try new foods all the time, just like my mom did. "Try it, you'll like it!" turns out to be a survival measure, passed on by mothers for literally a million years.

Dr. Briana Pobiner, a research scientist with the Smithsonian Institution and one of the people responsible for putting together the Human Origins exhibit, has studied the human evolution diet, in particular the Paleolithic diet from between 2.5 million and 1 million years ago, in eastern and southern parts of Africa. So of course, when I got the opportunity to speak with her, my first question was: "So, what do you think of the Paleo Diet?" She immediately laughed. (I guess she gets this question all the time.) Then she set the record straight:

> On the one hand, I really love the way this diet has elevated the field of paleoanthropology. Few people knew it existed before now! On the other hand, I find there are some real flaws with the Paleo Diet nutritionally. For example, the diet does not encourage eating grains or dairy, claiming that we have not evolved enough to digest them. This is not true, as we have clear genetic adaptations to both that date back at least several thousand years. My second issue with the diet is that it seems to assume that what our ancestors ate was always good for them. This was often not the case. Our early ancestors were often starving, eating poorly, and most died by the time they were 35 or 40.[5]

So fine, I guess we did not always have the best food choices way back when. But if we could go back in time, in an ideal world, what should we have put on the menu to best meet our energy needs?

Interestingly, modern-day hunter-gatherer societies (a proxy for understanding hunter-gatherers of long ago) tend to eat higher levels of protein than people in modern industrial societies, but it is unfair to say that there is a strict norm for how people should eat, either now or in the distant past. Some subsistence groups from arctic populations today have a diet almost exclusively consisting of animal material, and some small-scale farming societies subsist on a mix of plant and animal foods. The diversity of our diets is as diverse as we are as people. To quote Marlene Zuk, an evolutionary biologist and behavioral ecologist and author of *Paleofantasy*, "There was no single Paleo Lifestyle, any more than there is a single Modern Lifestyle. Early humans trapped or fished, relied on large game or small, or collected a large proportion of their food, depending on where in the world they lived and the time period in which they were living."[6]

The big difference, it seems, from the way we ate 2 million years ago versus today is that then, we spent an enormous amount of energy hunting and scavenging for fresh food, whereas today, our food is processed and comes to us by way of a grocery store. William Leonard, head of the Department of Anthropology at Northwestern University, and his colleagues estimate that based on modern hunter-gathering practices, our evolutionary grandparents walked or ran an average of 13.1 kilometers (8 miles) a day, looking for food. The other key aspect of physical activity in subsistence societies is the fact that much of the daily work was done at a slow to moderate pace versus high-intensity workouts.[7] These people slowly burned energy looking for food all day. So for most of human history, the work of hunting and scavenging was pretty much a full-time job.

Leonard also looked at the body mass index (BMI) of modern subsistence farmers, herders, and hunters. He found that among males, the mean BMIs for the subsistence groups ranged from 20.4 to 22.5, with the average for each group significantly less than that of industrialized nations. The patterns were similar for women.[8] Subsistence farmers tend to exercise more and throughout the day and eat just enough to support their lifestyle.

According to Leonard, early humans had "high physical energy expenditure and frequent periods of marginal or negative energy balance," meaning there was often more energy leaving than going into their bodies. They were thin because they ate a steady diet of nutrition-rich foods and burned off energy as they consumed it. At a certain point in history, however, the way we collected, prepared, and consumed food changed pretty dramatically. And the triggers for this are fascinating.

FARMING AND ANIMAL DOMESTICATION

Farming has been part of human existence for roughly 10,500 years. Its inception was an incredible moment in human history, when we no longer needed to run around all day looking for food to survive and could focus instead on transforming our surroundings by planting, watering, raising crops, and tending herds. A new way of life emerged, as we focused on growing agriculture and building cities. Paleoanthropologists believe that this transformative change happened for two big reasons. According to Richard Potts and Christopher Sloan, who wrote the companion book to the Smithsonian exhibit, *What Does It Mean to Be Human?*, "First was the suite of physical, mental, social and technological traits that had accumulated over the course of human evolution. Second was the rapidly thawing environment at the end of the last ice age, followed by a relatively stable climate."[9]

With a big break in the weather as the planet became warmer and wetter, we figured out how to domesticate cows in Africa and the Middle East (10,000 years ago), grow squash in Central America (10,000 years ago), cultivate corn in North America (9,000 years ago), and grow rice in China (9,000 years ago).[10] Almost at the same time worldwide, we leveraged all of the skills we had collected throughout our hunter-gather years—to make tools, hunt animals, cook, store food, and create huts, hearths, and clothing—and used them to become very good farmers. But we also became more planted in one place. No need to wander around looking for food if you can grow it easily in your backyard! So with domesticated plants and animals, all of our ancient cities were born, along with increased crop yields, drought tolerance, easier harvests, and better nutrition.

As incredible as it was from a food production of view, the movement to farming was not that easy. Living in close quarters and in more dense urban settings for the first time put people at risks for diseases and maladies they might not have had to deal with on the open range. Plus, it was very physically taxing. For example, a study was done in 2011 that gives us a glimpse of the level of exertion required by early small farmers in our evolutionary history. The study looked at the physical activity of Amish and non-Amish adults in Ohio Appalachia, measuring the number of steps they took. The researchers specifically looked at Amish farmers because their work is more labor-intensive than industrial agriculture practices today (they don't rely on modern equipment) and is more proximate to the way farmers might have worked in the distant past. Male Amish farmers took 15,278 steps (roughly 7 ½ miles) per day on average, whereas non-Amish men from the same area took 7,605 steps a day. (Interestingly, the study concluded that the farmers' higher levels of physical activity may be a contribution to lower cancer incidence rates documented among this Amish group.[11])

Farming was then and still is for some communities laborious dusk-till-dawn work, but with the increased number of domesticated animals, better tools, and eventually the invention of machines and industrial processes, life got a little easier. In fact, it was the Industrial Revolution that allowed some of us, for the first time in our evolutionary history, to stop thinking about "what's for dinner" all the time and instead explore the arts, sciences, and other pursuits not related to food gathering.

FACTORIES AND GIN CARTS

The Industrial Revolution came into full swing in the late 1700s and early 1800s, when almost every facet of daily life changed. Most economic historians agree that the onset of the Industrial Revolution was the most important event in the history of humanity since the domestication of animals, plants, and fire. The average income and the population began to exhibit unprecedented and sustained growth. How we produced food, clothing, and buildings changed, whole transportation systems were created, a professional middle class emerged, and the language of work changed. Terms like "productiveness" (circa 1727) and "productivity" (circa 1809)—words still in use today in business—were first used to describe a new way of thinking about how we create value. Work was no longer about what humans could do but what humans could do with the help of machines.

Factory buildings were perfect physical manifestations of the business theories and concepts they were supporting—in other words, of "productivity." Most of these buildings were efficiently organized, sizable, and open, designed with the latest technology at the time to beautifully accommodate machinery and to allow factory managers to observe the work being done by their vast labor force. However, the buildings were typically not designed so well for the health of workers who regularly inhaled coal fumes, put in 12+ hours a day performing monotonous tasks, and were forced to endanger themselves regularly to keep production levels high.

In the early 1700s in England, even before the Industrial Revolution was in full swing, gin carts (vending carts on wheels carrying gin) became popular in places like London and Manchester, rolling up and down the streets and even down factory floors to keep people working in these dismal conditions. And despite the miserable nature of the work for many factory laborers, and the fact that they were in large part alcoholics, their work did involve regular movement and exercising their bodies as part of their job. The good news is that through the 1800s and 1900s, several major labor movements put limits on the number of hours that could be worked, environmental laws improved air quality, business and building codes began protecting worker safety, machines were designed with ergonomics in mind, and people stopped drinking large amounts of gin (which had not exactly been good for laborers' safety working around large, sometimes dangerous machinery).

Also, in reaction to seeing the squalor and poor conditions of factory life, some business leaders began integrating the health of their workers into their business model as a way of keeping them fit, productive, and loyal to the company. For example, in 1888, the village of Port Sunlight, in Merseyside, England, was built by the Lever Brothers to accommodate workers in their soap factory. Port Sunlight included public buildings such as the Lady Lever Art Gallery, a cottage hospital, schools, a concert hall, an open air swimming pool, a church, and a temperance hotel (where no alcohol was served). Lever Brothers introduced welfare schemes and provided for the education and entertainment of their workforce, encouraging recreation and organizations that promoted art, literature, science, or music.

In the United States, around 1905, Milton Hershey built a chocolate factory with worker health and well-being in mind in what is now Hershey, Pennsylvania. Hershey created a completely new community around his factory including comfortable homes, a public transportation system, a quality public school system, and extensive recreational and cultural opportunities. Unlike other industrialists of his time, Hershey wanted to avoid building a faceless company town with row houses. He wanted a "real home town" with tree-lined streets, single- and two-family brick houses, and manicured lawns. He was concerned about providing adequate recreation and diversions for his employees and their families, so he built an amusement park that opened in 1907 and expanded rapidly over the next several years. This amusement park continues to be a strong part of the community, even today.

WORK IN THE 20TH CENTURY

The past 100 years have included major changes that have shifted how we work once again, and in fairly profound ways. We've gone from riding horseback to traveling on airplanes, from using pencils to iPads, from working in factories to hanging out in coworking facilities. In most industrialized countries, there has also been a shift from manufacturing-based businesses to service businesses. All of these changes are particularly fascinating to witness by peaking inside the buildings where people worked. In many ways, the buildings were a manifestation of the nature of work happening inside them. They still are. Let's look at some of the changes in office space over the last 100 years.

■ The "Factory" Office

In the early part of the 20th century, the first large office buildings looked and behaved a lot like factories. Only at this point, workers were not pushing machines; instead, they started pushing paper. The Larkin Building, designed by Frank Lloyd Wright and built in 1906 for the Larkin Soap Company in Buffalo, New York, was a great illustration of innovation in many ways. The five-story dark red brick fortress of a building had air conditioning, stained glass windows, built-in desk furniture, and suspended toilet bowls (designed by Wright so that the floors were easier to clean). As innovative as this building was, it looked and felt like a factory, especially in the large atrium space full of rows of workers performing administrative work. (See Figure 2-1.)

Figure 2-1. The interior of the Larkin Building, designed by Frank Lloyd Wright.

▪ The Office Tower

As building technology improved and big business continued to blossom in cities, a number of very tall and very wide office buildings appeared. Many of these buildings appeared in New York City at the beginning of the 20th century—like the Metropolitan Life Tower (1909), Woolworth Building (1913), and Chrysler Building (1930)—but they popped up in every major city in the coming decades. To give you a sense of scale, the Empire State Building in New York, completed in 1931, includes 2.25 million square feet of occupied space, which, as of 2007, housed roughly 1,000 companies and 21,000 people. What this meant at a practical level for those working in these spaces is that they were surrounded by a busy hive of people day in and day out.

Jack Lemmon, in the movie *The Apartment* (1960), was supposed to have worked for a "large insurance company," likely modeled after the interior space of one of these large buildings. (See Figure 2-2.) Just imagine even more paper pushers, shoved together, sitting at open desks with enclosed offices surrounding the perimeter of the space cutting off all natural light. Then add in lots of noise created by people shouting on phones, the clacking of typewriters, and wafts of cigarette smoke everywhere, and you get a sense of what work was like in these buildings.

▪ Cube Farms

Then, in the 1960s, the cubicle was born. This new kind of open office was introduced by a few designers, but most notably Robert Propst from Herman Miller, a large furniture manufacturer. The initial design idea for the cubicle was to provide more productivity, privacy, and health in the open environment, and to allow workers to easily configure or reconfigure their work area with modular elements such as work surfaces,

Figure 2-2. Scene from the movie *The Apartment*.

Figure 2-3. Herman Miller's Action Office furniture system.

overhead bins, drawers, and shelving. The first Propst cubicle designs, called Action Office in 1968, had varying heights and surfaces. (See Figure 2-3.) Over time, cubicles became more regular and efficient in shape, taller, and the butt of Dilbert cartoon jokes. Probst later claimed that "The cubiclizing of people in modern corporations is monolithic insanity."[12]

■ The Mobile Office

In the early 1990s, largely because of the incredible influence of mobile technology (laptops, tablets, cell phones, etc.), it became possible to work away from the office, untethered from a cubicle, and instead work virtually with coworkers. Full-time homeworking increased in popularity as did telecommuting (working part time from home) and working in satellite offices. Employees no longer had to be in the same place or even work at the same time as their teammates. As an example, in 1992, the federal government began piloting a series of interagency satellite offices for workers in and around Washington, DC, to enable telework and reduce congestion and workers' commutes into the city.

From a health and wellness perspective, the transformation of our work style over the last several decades, from factory to cubicle to home (either full time or on occasion), has impacted our health for good and for bad. On the positive side, office buildings and public spaces everywhere are now relatively smoke-free, and ergonomics have emerged as a multidisciplinary profession and resource.[13] We also have more choice than ever in how we work individually and in groups, to suit different personalities, skills, and preferences. Unfortunately, these changes in our work and our work environment are also impacting our health in negative ways.

A study of occupations done by Dr. Tim Church from the Pennington Biomedical Research Center and others compared levels of physical activity for the entire American workforce over the past five decades. They found that workers in 2010 burned fewer calories, on average, than people in previous generations, purely based on the increased prevalence of more sedentary jobs. According to their findings, "Over the last 50 years in the U.S., we estimate that daily occupation-related energy expenditure has decreased by more than 100 calories, and this reduction in energy expenditure accounts for a significant portion of the increase in mean U.S. body weights for women and men." Back in the early 1960s, almost half of private industry occupations in the United States required at least moderate-intensity physical activity. Today, 80 percent of Americans have jobs that are classified as sedentary or require very light physical activity.[14]

WORKING TODAY

Fast forward to today. A significant part of the research I do as a workplace specialist involves observing people in workplaces—otherwise known as *workplace anthropology*. It is a technique that assesses how people space is used by tracking people in space with technology, following people around, and lots of observing. It is amazing what you can learn about work patterns and behavior, even when people are not around to tell you what is happening. Using data within the past few years from observations of roughly 40,000 work points (i.e., offices, workstations, bench seats, conference rooms, break areas, cafeterias, etc.), survey data from 23,000 people globally, and a few other sources, here is a quick summary of work life today for knowledge workers.[15]

▪ The Hours We Work

Workers in the United States and Canada clock in 1,705 hours a year, which is slightly more than workers in the UK (1,650), France (1,476), and Germany (1,406) but significantly less than in Taiwan (2,144) or Singapore (2,287).[16] At least that is what we put on our timesheets. Many of us also put in extra unbooked hours. A survey put out by Good Technology, a mobility security company, found that some 80 percent of the 1,000 Americans polled said they spend 7 extra hours a week, or 30 extra hours a month, checking emails and answering phone calls after hours.[17] So for years, laborers in countries everywhere fought hard to limit our workweek to 40 hours, and almost instantaneously with the invention of mobile technology, we threw this right out the window.

■ Where Work Happens

Most knowledge workers are sitting in their office only 52 percent of the time. The rest of the time they are in a conference room, the cafeteria, working at home, on a plane, on a train, in a hotel, or on a grocery line. If someone asked you "Are you a mobile worker?" you can probably say yes. You are mobile because you work in lots of places throughout your day and week. That is also likely true as well if you work in a school, a hospital, an airport, or any profession that requires working in more than one primary location. That said, just because you are mobile does not mean you are actually moving. Our work has actually become much more sedentary since we have been tethered to our beloved electronic devices.

■ What We Do While Working

When knowledge workers are in the office, they spend 37 percent of their day, on average, collaborating. Most of that collaboration time is spent collaborating with others remotely (web-, tele-, or videoconference meetings), and a surprisingly small amount of collaboration time is spent in face-to-face meetings. Of course, a number of organizations encourage people to get together and talk in person more often, but you would be surprised how little this actually happens today. More likely than not, we are collaborating through some sort of device. Also, most office workers sit the majority of the time they are working. Studies vary, but on average, office workers have been found to sit 68 to 82 percent of an eight-hour day. Even jobs where you would think people would not sit so much—like being a teacher or working in a lab, for example—can require significant paperwork, research, analysis, etc., which requires sitting for many hours at a time.

Our Eating Habits at Work

Only a third of American workers say they take a lunch break, and 65 percent of workers eat at their desks or do not take a break at all, according to a Web survey conducted by Right Management, a human resources consulting firm.[18] Those eating while working probably ate more and felt less full after a meal than their nondistracted coworkers who were exclusively focused on eating.[19] Eating while you work is not just bad for digestion. You actually eat more and get hungrier later.

And what about all of that snacking from vending machines? In 2012, the vending business in the United States reached $19 billion, with 22.5 percent of sales in manufacturing facilities, 21.1 percent in offices, and 6.6 percent in hospitals.[20] Vending machines are so prevalent and so impactful to our diet that the Food and Drug Administration announced that in an effort to combat obesity, roughly 5 million vending machines nationwide were required to display calorie information starting in 2014 as part of the Affordable Care Act.[21]

What the Workplace Looks Like

Offices built for knowledge workers today (versus those built more than 10 years ago) tend to dedicate fewer square feet to individual offices, with more space for collaborative areas and amenities (like nap rooms, telephone booths, quiet rooms, cafeterias, training rooms, and break areas). These additional spaces are designed to be places for working, not just talking about sports or what your kids are doing, though this informal discussion is helpful for building business relationships. In general, having more choice in where you work is a good thing for productivity, for satisfaction, and for supporting the varied nature of knowledge work and the increase in mobility (which we will dig into deeper in Chapter 3). Unfortunately, many of the buildings where work happens today are still designed like factories from the Industrial Revolution. They might be tightly packed, dark, or have poor indoor air quality. They might provide only one way to work (sitting glued to one seat) without any ability to adjust furniture, lighting, or equipment to respond to the human need to walk, sit, stand, or even rest during the workday.

■ Who Is Working Today

For the first time in history, up to five generations are actually living at the same time, which is a medical miracle in itself, but we are also working together in the same organization. And though most people in the veteran generation (born before 1946) have retired by this point, we can't assume people from the Baby Boomer generation (born between 1946 and 1964) will retire anytime soon. In fact, if you ask Boomers when they are going to retire, chances are they will be offended by the question. The result is that more people are expanding the number of years they choose to work. Long term, we can assume that a larger percentage of the workforce will suffer more and longer from ailments caused by unhealthy work practices if we don't change our work style now.

☯

In summary, office work patterns today are extremely boring and not exactly healthy by anyone's standard. Believe me, I've been watching you! When my team performs workplace observations, sometimes we have to overload on coffee just to make it through our research. Every once in a while I would just love to see someone break out in song with a set of resistance bands or go running through the halls, just to make this part of my job a little more exciting. With the exception of going to the bathroom or grabbing coffee every now and then, most office workers are glued to their desk, mindlessly eating and talking or typing on devices. I'm sure they are aware there is a gym, an outdoor area, or a nice break room, but they don't use these very much because, well, that is often not perceived as productive time. That said, what is productivity anyway? It seems like that term is thrown around quite a bit, but what is our connection to it and is it even the right term to explain the output of our work today?

Before we dive into the details of how to increase productivity, it's worth first understanding the term a little more. When I'm designing a new workplace or coming up with a workplace strategy for an organization, leaders often state that one of their key goals is "to increase the productivity of their employees." When I ask what that means, I have found that the answer varies widely based on industry, on job function, even on the individual. It's important to put a stake in the ground and define what it means to be productive today, so that solutions for improving productivity (and health) are put into context. The language and definitions we use are important, especially when making the business case for changing organizational, team, and individual behaviors.

3

Productivity, Flow, and Creativity

T HE WORD *PRODUCTIVITY*, AS MENTIONED earlier, was first used during the Industrial Revolution; later, around 1899, it was defined specifically in economic terms as "an increase in the rate of output per unit." The equation calculates input as labor and capital and output as revenues and other components in gross domestic product like business inventories. Over time, the meaning of the word *productivity* has expanded to include microeconomic and macroeconomic theory and to incorporate differences across industries. For example, capital spent on equipment for a car manufacturer is a major input, whereas people might be the largest productivity input for a consulting firm.

And even though capital spent on equipment and goods is still really important for many industries (car manufacturers, energy companies, etc.), it is fair to say that people, affectionately referred to as *human capital*, are the largest input to productivity globally and a critical factor for the future growth of our global economy. Especially as the services sector becomes larger and larger, people become a larger percentage of the economic engine. According to the World Bank, service industries in highly industrialized countries represent 66 percent of the world economy, while manufacturing is 32 percent and agriculture is 2 percent.[1]

But it's not just the shift to the service economy that is putting the pressure on human capital as the primary input for growth. There is also an increase in the need for knowledge workers, or people with high levels of expertise, education, or experience—people whose jobs involve the creation, distribution, or application of knowledge, such as software developers, doctors, lawyers, inventors, teachers, financial analysts, and architects. As businesses continue to increase their dependence on technology, and in particular information technology, the number of fields in which knowledge workers operate continues to expand. And because of this trend, there is a shift from focusing on *productivity,* or the means of production, and instead putting an emphasis on outcomes and *performance.* The point here is that businesses are becoming more dependent on their workers and for those workers to perform at a high level, not just push paper around. A company needs people working at their peak performance to run the business, grow it, divest it, reinvent it, and then grow it some more.

So how do employers maximize their investment in human capital and supercharge all those knowledge workers they employ? How do companies create the right environment and "headspace" for individuals and groups of all kinds to maximize not just their performance but also to tap into their most creative, most innovative thinking? It turns out there are common triggers for this, some of which are illustrated by the concepts of flow, group flow, and the unique elements that spawn creativity.

FLOW

When people are most efficient and effective, they are in a state of flow, sometimes also referred to as "being in the zone" or "being in the groove." Flow refers to a state of total absorption in a given activity, to the point where time seems to slow or stop and self-consciousness is greatly diminished. This is a state of being completely engaged in something to the point of being in a near meditative state. People can experience flow when they are doing creative activities that utilize individual special strengths, like writing, painting, speaking, or even number crunching. Certain aspects of people's jobs can lend themselves to flow, and when they experience it often, their work tends to bring greater job satisfaction.

The concept of flow was first studied by Mihaly Csikszentmihalyi and illustrated in his book *Flow: The Psychology of Optimal Experience*. Csikszentmihalyi, who is a Distinguished Professor of Psychology and Management at Claremont Graduate University, describes the flow state as one in which an athlete or individual performs at his or her best, seemingly without effort, but with total concentration, feeling totally in control without thinking about it. Self-consciousness recedes into the background as total focus is upon present activity. Flow is completely focused motivation. In flow, the emotions are not just contained and channeled, but more positive, energized, and aligned with the task at hand. The hallmark of flow is a feeling of spontaneous joy, even rapture, while performing a task. Csikszentmihalyi identifies a number of factors needed to create flow, including "an intense and focused concentration on the present moment," "the merging of action and awareness," and "a sense of personal control or agency over the situation or activity."[2]

The most dramatic examples of flow come from sports, particularly high-risk sports. In Steven Kotler's *The Rise of Superman: Decoding the Science of Ultimate Human Performance*, he shares story after story of incredible physical and mental feats achieved by surfers, skiers, skateboarders, BASE jumpers—all tapping into their flow state and achieving something that had never been done before.[3] So flow does not just help us feel good and be productive. It can also help us achieve great innovative or creative feats.

A workplace that supports flow can vary by individual preference, so accommodating flow requires some flexibility from a management perspective as well as allowing employees to pick and choose the environment that works best for the task at hand. As an example, some people find flow in an enclosed, quiet space to work while others prefer the background noise and the buzz of a coffee shop. It is also critical for technology, equipment, and other materials to be available so that there are fewer barriers to making flow happen.

Though many professions require a certain amount of flow for individual work, there are few people who depend on it more than those who write for a living. Interestingly, many writers seem to have honed their work environment over the years to capture their flow experience beautifully. David McCullough is an American author, narrator, historian, and lecturer. He has twice won both the Pulitzer Prize and the National Book Award and is a recipient of the Presidential Medal of Freedom, the highest civilian award in the United States. His books *John Adams* and *Truman* have both been turned into an HBO film and a mini-series respectively. McCullough has written all of these great works in a tiny shed in the backyard behind his house in Martha's Vineyard. Known as "the bookshop," the shed does not have a telephone or running water. Its primary contents are a typewriter, a green banker's lamp, a desk, and a few books and papers. To keep from being startled while working, McCullough asks his family members to whistle as they approach the shed when he is writing.[4]

In the modern office workplace, we can replicate workspaces like McCullough's writing shed with well-designed cellular offices, including walls, views to the outdoors, and good design that minimizes foot traffic and disruption. The problem, of course, is that most jobs today require us to work as individuals, yes, but also to do a sizable amount of work with other people, in teams. The reality is that most of us need work environments, technologies, and business protocols that support group flow, not just individual flow.

GROUP FLOW

Keith Sawyer, researcher and author of *Group Genius: The Creative Power of Collaboration,* built on Csikszentmihalyi's work and hacked into the working patterns of great comedians, jazz groups, and other creative teams to develop specific elements needed for creating *group* flow. Many of these patterns overlap with the same conditions required for individual flow, including "complete concentration" and "being in control." But other group-specific elements include "a compelling vision and shared mission," "a blending of egos," a "familiarity with teammates," and "constant communication."[5]

In business, some of the best examples of group flow come from small start-up companies or small teams within larger organizations that have autonomy and limited hierarchy within the organization. Some of my best personal experiences of group flow have been with project design teams where all of the elements mentioned above were in place but also where team members could practically read each other's minds and felt completely comfortable with each other's work styles. These relationships developed because the teams worked (and played) together over long periods of time, had super clear goals, and had the authority to adapt what we were doing during the course of a project. Our sense of flow was also enhanced by the physical environment we occupied. We had access to whiteboards, flexible team rooms, and all the tools we needed to support the work at hand.

A workplace environment that supports group flow is likely controlled by the team using it, is flexible, and is "open" (with no, or low, walls) at least to members of the group. These workplaces also allow for some improvisation or movement of furniture, equipment, or technology and do not emphasize hierarchy. An example of a space that supports group flow well is the Center for the Sciences & Innovation (CSI) at Trinity University in San Antonio, Texas. This is a unique place on the campus where students from such departments as biology, computer science, and engineering, as well as from the arts, business, and other areas of study, take classes and come together for special projects and to create new business ideas.

The CSI building (see Figures 3-1 and 3-2) is actually made of three kinds of spaces that support group flow—one type for thinking and brainstorming, a second type for modeling or designing prototypes of product ideas in a computer lab environment, and a third type for physically making products in a two-story, open, airy space called The Cube. In this large "maker space," all of the furniture is on wheels and can be easily adjusted and adapted for professors and student groups. Custom mobile work stations were designed for student groups of three to six that include a whiteboard, a butcher-block tabletop, flat-screen display, power outlets, data ports, storage (for tools, supplies, and student backpacks), and a compartment to house electronic equipment hardwired into the design station. These stations can be moved around if needed.[6] Also, one of the walls in The Cube has three garage doors that can be opened up to the outdoors so that equipment can be rolled outside if it is too large to move through a door.

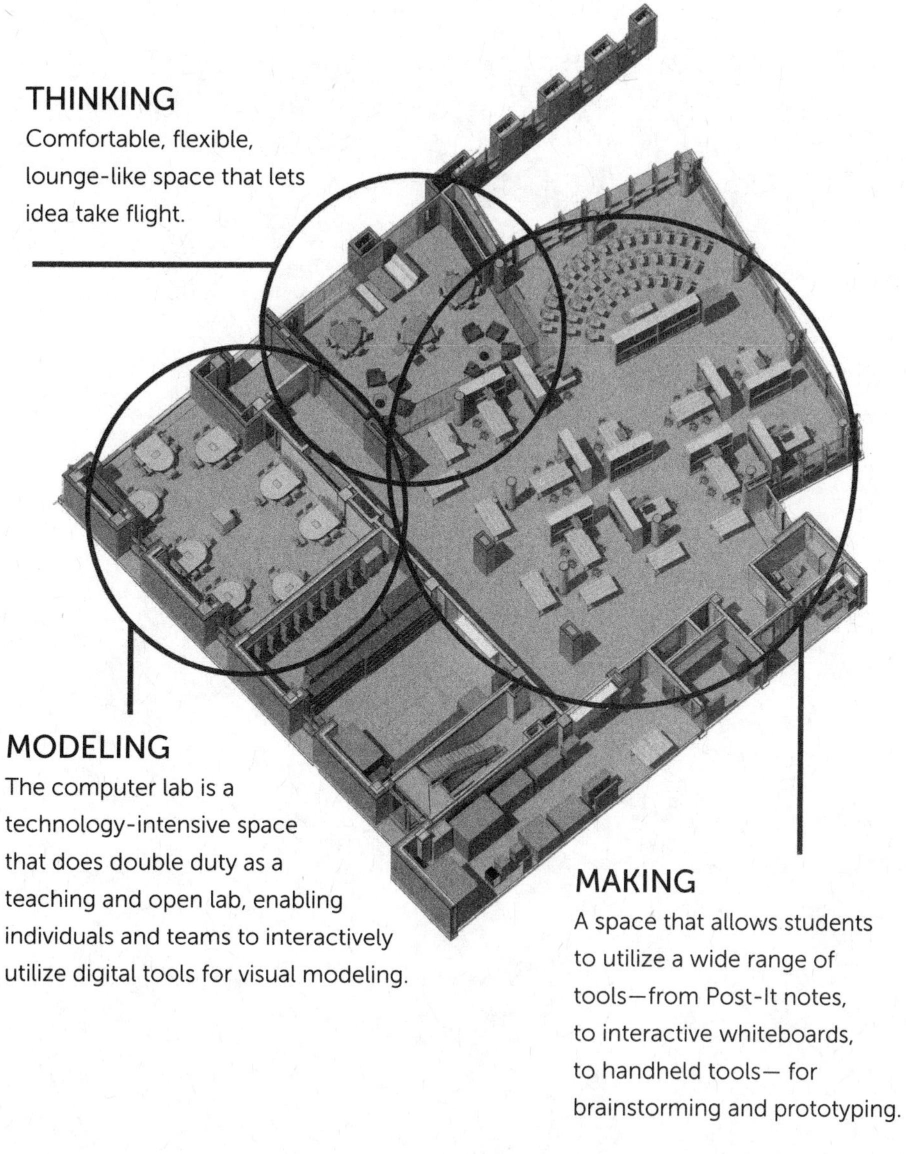

THINKING
Comfortable, flexible, lounge-like space that lets idea take flight.

MODELING
The computer lab is a technology-intensive space that does double duty as a teaching and open lab, enabling individuals and teams to interactively utilize digital tools for visual modeling.

MAKING
A space that allows students to utilize a wide range of tools—from Post-It notes, to interactive whiteboards, to handheld tools— for brainstorming and prototyping.

Figure 3-1. Thinking, modeling, and making spaces at the Center for the Sciences & Innovation, Trinity University, San Antonio, Texas, designed by EYP. Image courtesy of EYP.

Figure 3-2. "The Cube" maker space at the Center for the Sciences & Innovation, Trinity University, San Antonio, Texas, designed by EYP. Image courtesy of EYP, ©Tim Griffith.

According to David Ribble, professor of biology at Trinity, who served as a key client contact on the design team, "The really beautiful thing about the space is what happens between formally scheduled classes and events. Students are in there studying, others are working on a whiteboard, a few others are building something. It's a very vibrant space." The building was designed to facilitate learning and entrepreneurial activity from all across the campus, and the curriculum at the university also changed and evolved to support this more collaborative model. Ribble believes these changes and the space itself have helped integrate faculty and even entire departments to some extent. "It is so easy for us to come into work and stay in our office or lab all day," he says. "But the whole social climate of academics is critically important. It's important for the students, and it makes us better teachers and scholars. Having a building like this helps us all to engage our social mind."[7]

CREATIVITY

Businesses today thrive based on their ability to constantly streamline processes, create new products and services, and reinvent themselves. This requires a heavy dose of creativity from the employees that run them. And not just from employees in traditionally "creative" fields like design, art, music, and film, but from all fields including research, science, law, engineering, accounting, and finance. As humans, our ability to think creatively is a unique competitive advantage and important for driving our economy. An IBM survey of more than 1,500 CEOs from 60 countries and 33 industries worldwide found that these leaders believe that "more than rigor, management discipline, integrity or even vision—successfully navigating an increasingly complex world will require creativity."[8] But what does being creative really entail? This is where some of the latest research gets interesting. Experts in psychology and neuroscience have been exploring creativity to define the triggers that spark insights and innovation and how our brain responds to them. These insights can impact how we think about work and the workplace.

Relaxation and Movement

Through his research on what are called *predictive brain signals*, Joydeep Bhattacharya, PhD—a psychologist at Goldsmiths, University of London—finds that the brain is most likely to gain insight with a steady rhythm of alpha waves emanating from the right hemisphere. These alpha waves are closely associated with relaxing activities such as walking, taking a warm shower, even drinking alcohol. Bhattacharya claims that when we are intensely focused on a task, we are least likely to have an insight.[9] This may seem counterintuitive, because most of us tend to hunker down and increase our focus when we are trying to work through a difficult problem. In reality, though, a "clenched state of mind" inhibits the connections in the brain that can lead to creative breakthroughs. Given that most workers are not able to take a shower or drink alcohol at work (no more gin carts, sorry), walking is probably a better choice to engage those creative juices.

According to a study coauthored by Marily Oppezzo, a Stanford doctoral graduate in educational psychology, and Daniel Schwartz, dean of the Stanford Graduate School of Education, reactive thinking improves during walking and shortly thereafter. Their study found that walking indoors or outdoors similarly boosted creative inspiration. The act of walking itself, and not the environment, was the main factor. Across the board, creativity levels were consistently and significantly higher for those walking compared to those sitting.[10] Walking has also been shown to help with improved attention and short-term recall.[11]

■ The Need for Face-to-Face Collisions

But walking, by itself, is not always a recipe for creating radical new ideas. For that, we need to bump into people and break out of our comfort zone a bit. Here is where the work of Geoffrey West comes into play. West is a British theoretical physicist at the Santa Fe Institute who is one of the leading scientists in the behavior and patterns of cities. After years of collecting data, West and his colleague, Luis Bettencourt, discovered that just about every socioeconomic variable, from the production of patents to per capita income, could be described with just a few simple equations. They used those equations to calculate productivity at an urban scale. Interestingly, they found that productivity increased by the size of the city, and as the size of the city doubled, productivity increased by a factor of 1.15. For example, a person in a city of 1 million will generate, on average, about 15 percent more patents and make 15 percent more in salary than a person living in a city of 500,000. The bigger the city, the more productivity per capita. According to West, "Cities are this inexhaustible source of ideas, and that's entirely because of these equations. As cities get bigger, everything starts accelerating." But it's not just size that matters, apparently; density does too. West's research shows that the most creative cities are the ones with the most collisions between people. According to Jonah Lehrer, a science writer and author of *Imagine: How Creativity Works*, this density is sometimes referred to as "urban friction."[12]

West eventually translated the work he was doing for cities and applied it to modern corporations. He discovered that corporate productivity, unlike urban productivity, didn't increase with size. In fact, the opposite happened. As the number of employees grew, the amount of profit per employee shrank. According to West, this decrease in per capita production is rooted in a failure of innovation. Instead of imitating the city, he suggests that businesses often minimize the very interactions that lead to new ideas, erecting walls and establishing hierarchies, stifling conversations, discouraging dissent, and suffocating social networks. Rather than maximizing employee creativity, companies become obsessed with minor efficiencies. It seems that the very thing that would help organizations increase their value—creativity and innovation—is being stifled by their desire to control how collaboration happens and put everything into its own box.

Thomas Allen, professor of organization studies at the MIT Sloan School of Management, has been studying how collaboration and creativity work within buildings, with a particular focus on proximity. One of his studies found that people are less likely to communicate face-to-face during the week when their workplaces are more than 30 meters (roughly 100 feet) from each other. When distances are longer than that, people default to phone calls, email, or other means of communication. He suggests that people who really need to communicate with each other to discuss complex or abstract ideas should do so face-to-face, and to facilitate this, they should sit by each other. He also recommends positioning work groups near each other when they have the most potential to spark strategic creativity in each other, and this should be prioritized over positioning groups near each other whose members are most likely to be working together now.[13] Workplaces that are organized strategically recognize the importance of clustering the right people together in order to maximize collaboration and creativity.

■ Innovation Districts

Interestingly, and almost in response to the need for urban friction and proximity, a number of *innovation districts* have started to pop up in cities across the globe. Innovation districts— sometimes referred to as innovation quarters, innovation neighborhoods, or innovation corridors—are tight geographic areas where leading-edge anchor institutions and companies cluster and connect with start-ups, business incubators, and accelerators.

Innovation districts are physically compact, transit-accessible, and technically wired. They offer mixed-use housing, office, and retail. They offer workers and the people who live there a great walkable lifestyle, but they also bring together the right elements for business innovation and creativity. Innovation districts include entrepreneurs, educational institutions, start-ups, mixed-use development, medical innovations, bike-sharing, and bankable investments. Why are they appearing? According to the Brookings Institution:

> [A] rising number of innovative firms and talented workers are choosing to congregate and co-locate in compact, amenity-rich enclaves in the cores of central cities. Rather than building on green-field sites, marquee companies in knowledge-intensive sectors are locating key facilities close to other firms, research labs, and universities so that they can share ideas and practice "open innovation."[14]

These sites have the right blend of economic, physical, and networking assets. When these three elements combine with a supportive, risk-taking culture, they create an *innovation ecosystem*—a synergistic relationship between people, groups, and place (the physical geography of the district) that facilitates idea generation and accelerates commercialization. You can find these innovative areas in Barcelona, Spain; Berlin, Germany; Cambridge, Massachusetts; London, England; Montreal, Canada; Philadelphia, Pennsylvania; Seoul, South Korea; Stockholm, Sweden; Toronto, Canada; and many other cities.[15]

Creative companies have taken these principles to heart by making changes to their physical work environment and endorsing behaviors in the workplace that support relaxation, movement, and the informal blending of ideas across organizational boundaries, as well as moving closer to partner organizations in order to realize a larger vision. It almost seems counterintuitive, but sitting in a chair all day—or exclusively hanging out in the office—is not the way to achieve the best business outcomes.

PERSONAL CONTROL AND CHOICE

Flow, group flow, and creativity all require a number of factors to make us effective, but one of the common factors, and a particularly important one, is that we have a certain degree of choice or control over the way we work. Without this choice or control, we become stressed and our performance suffers.

Robert Karasek, an industrial engineer and sociologist, and Tores Theorell, a specialist in industrial medicine, have been studying stress and jobs for a long time. Their epidemiological studies over decades have carefully measured the stress level of hundreds of jobs and the impact of those jobs on the health of workers (particularly heart disease). They created a model that organizes each job they have studied using two factors: (1) the levels of "psychological demands" of the job, and (2) the "decision latitude" or control of the worker to manage how he or she could deal with psychological demands. The results of their studies show that those workers with the greatest risk for illness are those with *high psychological demands and low decision latitude*. In other words, if you have a job that does not provide much choice in how you are able to manage stress, you are more likely to suffer mentally and physically. Theorell describes how workers who have control over their work and work environment typically have more positive health outcomes, even if they have stressful jobs:

The combination of high psychological demand and high decision latitude is defined as the *active* situation. In this situation, the worker has been given more resources to cope with high psychological demands because he/she can make relevant decisions, such as planning working hours according to his/her own biological rhythm. In addition, he/she has greater possibilities to improve coping strategies—facilitating feelings of mastery and control in unforeseen situations. This situation corresponds to psychological growth.[16]

Karasek and Theorell describe how jobs can be adjusted to better balance choice and stress today, such as providing employees with skills education or training, increasing their decision authority, and possibly decreasing the psychological demands of their job. In their book *Healthy Work: Stress, Productivity, and the Reconstruction of Working Life*, they describe ideal jobs as ones that, beyond material rewards, "give workers influence over the selection of work routines such as working at home or flexible hours" and "have routine demands mixed with a liberal element of new learning challenges."[17] So, regardless of our profession or position, some choice as to where, when, and how we work can greatly impact flow, creativity, engagement, health, and the bottom line.

My colleagues and I recently did a study for a global financial services firm, including a survey of more than 9,000 respondents from 18 locations across the globe. On average, and consistently, 68 percent of the respondents across locations and service lines believed the company's flexible work policies (allowing them to work where, when, and how they need to) made them more effective. Specifically, the respondents believed that flexible work helped them to be effective serving their clients, to work more effectively on individual tasks, to better manage their professional/personal life, and to be more effective when collaborating with others.[18]

Sally Augustin, PhD, a noted environmental psychologist, claims, "When we don't feel in control of what happens to us in a place, we are stressed, discouraged, and frustrated. Feeling in control is the key here; we don't have to actually exercise control to reap psychological benefits."[19] In other words, just knowing that we can adjust our work and environment to better suit our needs makes a huge difference in how we feel about work and our ability to be productive.

The good news is that now, more than ever, we have choices about where, when, and how we work. Technology is small and mobile, our need for paper is being reduced significantly, and managers everywhere are learning how to handle virtual teams. Most companies have adopted some form of alternative work policy for those functions that can be performed out of the office or in a nontraditional way. Even when employees are in the office, they are given choices beyond just one setting in which to work. There is a new vocabulary that has emerged as part of the phenomenon of flexibility and individual control in the workplace, such as activity-based settings (a variety of work settings assigned to a group to share) and coworking space (where space is provided by a third party for a portion or all of one's work, and space may be reserved through technology for an hour, a day. or even months at a time).[20]

This "choice" idea, especially in terms of workplace provisioning, is really taking hold. In a recent survey of 538 organizations my colleagues and I conducted for the International Facility Management Association (IFMA), significant percentages of respondents claimed they are already using or about to roll out the use of touchdown spaces, activity-based settings, shared addresses, hoteling, group addresses, and free addresses in their workspaces.[21] In this same IFMA survey, respondents were asked why they are exploring new ways of provisioning employees, both on- and off-site. The responses were consistent. Companies are adopting these new policies to support work-life balance for employees, flexibility, aligning with organizational goals, aligning with advances in technology, and the perceived benefit to workers. Cost savings and real estate size reduction were also important drivers for trying something new (and an important part of the business case), but cost was chosen less often as a reason than organizational or employee-driven goals.[22] Even with all of this trending data, culturally, there is still sometimes a stigma for working differently, in a more "mobile" fashion, or away from a primary workplace, but the tides are turning as work flexibility helps companies recruit and retain the best and the brightest employees.

☯

And so now you have some context for what it means to be productive in today's world. This context is important because our work, and what is expected of us, is continuing to evolve. Workplaces that were effective even a few years ago are not necessarily so today. So what does make them effective? How can we design a workplace that best supports worker performance, flow, creativity, and choice? And what are specific ways that we can change behaviors, policies, business processes, technologies, and the environment to not only support work performance but also maximize human health, engagement, and happiness in a way that is sustainable? The next several chapters cover this on many levels, but let's start with our most valuable currency at work: our energy.

Maximize Energy, Avoid Crashes

D R. JIM LOEHR AND DR. Jack Groppel from the Johnson & Johnson Human Performance Institute, mentioned in Chapter 1, train elite athletes and are now using their findings to train the rest of us. Their Corporate Athlete® course covers many of the things you might expect a health and wellness training course to include, like tips on how to address nutrition, exercise, and stress reduction in the workplace. But the real "secret sauce" of their methodology is a focus on managing energy. Loehr and Groppel started studying human energy production at the cellular level, which led them to develop a very prescriptive program for exercise, nutrition intake, stress management, and other forms of recovery throughout the day. Their strategies are founded on a few key principles, which bring together *energy management* and *employee engagement*.

Most people think of energy as an infinite resource, but to fuel yourself for optimum performance and operate your mind and body as a well-oiled machine, it's important to replenish energy as you spend it throughout the day. We can't just fuel up at 7 a.m. and expect to be at peak performance for seven, eight, or nine hours straight. During any workday, we are bombarded by stressors, some small, some fairly significant. We are continually oscillating between stress and recovery. If we keep up long periods of giving our energy away without putting in place any strategies to restore it, we suffer from burnout and harm our health.

Loehr defines employee engagement with energy in mind. "Full engagement requires the conscious recruitment of all dimensions of energy—physical, emotional, mental, and spiritual," he says. "It represents the greatest quantity, highest quality, most precise focus, and greatest intensity of effort invested in whatever we are doing at the time." So we can be fully engaged at all levels when we manage our energy well. Here are some of the key principles around energy management:

▶ *Energy, not time, is the fundamental currency of high performance.* It is not the amount of time you invest in a project that drives success, but rather the energy you bring to the time you have. Time has value only in its intersection with energy.

▶ *Deepening employee engagement is essentially an energy management challenge.* Managing energy, managing engagement, and managing effort are functionally equivalent.

▶ *Human energy and engagement are not single-faceted.* By learning to manage the physical, emotional, mental, and spiritual aspects of energy more efficiently and effectively, employees' performance, health, and happiness can be significantly enhanced.

During the Corporate Athlete® course I took, most of the executives participating did a lot of nodding and commenting with personal stories as these principles were laid out for us. They appreciated the fact that science was behind the concepts presented, with "not a lot of health and wellness fluff." They felt that having the science behind the health would get the attention of business leaders and would be the difference between those leaders saying "That's a good idea" and "Let's do something about this now."

Some of the more tangible lessons we learned and applied during the course were designed to help us keep energy levels more even throughout the workday, such as eating well-portioned meals, eating regular healthy snacks, and integrating movement and exercise. These strategies have been woven into this chapter.

THE BENEFITS OF MOVEMENT

There is a great deal of noise in the media today about "step counting" and the importance of movement, so when I got the opportunity to interview Catrine Tudor-Locke, PhD— professor and department chair of kinesiology at the University of Massachusetts–Amherst—I was particularly excited. Tudor-Locke is kind of a rock star when it comes to the health of walking and is considered the "queen of step counters." One of her many claims to fame is the fact that she is the brains behind the recommended target number of steps we need to be healthy every day, which vary based on age and/or if we have a chronic disease.[1]

On the day I interviewed her by phone, she answered with a friendly hello and immediately asked, "Hey, can you give me a minute? I need to move to my treadmill." Of course. Our call was a task she could do while walking, and knowing all she does about the health benefits of walking, I could tell she did not want to lose any opportunity for extra activity. Tudor-Locke spent the next hour walking at a two mph pace and filling my head with facts. "The minimum threshold for steps a day is 7,500—that will get you in the game," she said. "Ten thousand steps a day is better from a public health perspective, and you should accumulate at least 3,000 of that at a three mph pace." Tudor-Locke loves the treadmill in her office and tries to do as many tasks while walking as possible. I asked her how she weaves steps into her day. "I can't draw, but can read, write, and do analyses on the treadmill, and I have three dogs, which helps me get a minimum of 12,000 to 14,000 steps a day."[2]

Tudor-Locke and many other academics across the globe lately have been on a tear, proving that sitting or even standing still for long periods of time is not healthy. Her research shows that changing positions is important as well as expending energy through movement on a regular basis. "If you sit all day, you reduce your energy expenditure and things are moving slowly through your body. Even if you replace a portion of your sitting day with walking, you are helping with energy expenditure," she says.

But how much walking should we do to be our healthy best? Turns out this is all about the number, intensity, and regularity of our steps.[3]

> *Number of steps.* Tudor-Locke and her colleagues created a pedometer-determined physical activity index for healthy adults with a range from those in a "sedentary lifestyle" category, who take fewer than 5,000 steps a day, to "highly active" groups, who regularly take more than 12,500 steps a day. Sadly, most U.S. adults walk only 6,500 steps per day on average, which falls into the "low active" classification of the index. Not ideal for reducing the risks of sedentary behavior.

> *Intensity of steps.* It is not just the number of steps we take a day that is important for a healthy lifestyle. It is also the intensity of those steps. Recommendations vary slightly, but most claim that for adults between the ages of 20 and 65, 3,000 to 4,000 of our daily steps (or a total of 15,000 steps a week) should be at a brisk pace (100 steps per minute, qualifying as moderate to vigorous

exercise). These brisk steps should be done for at least 10 minutes at a time and might include speed walking, running, biking, or working out on an elliptical machine.

▶ *Regularity of steps.* To really counter the negative health impacts of long hours of sedentary behavior—you know, reducing the risk of cardio metabolic conditions like diabetes, heart disease, stroke, and deep vein thrombosis—you should get up and stretch your legs (or even just stand) every 20 to 30 minutes and do some walking every 90 to 120 minutes. Unless you work for just two hours a day, this means moving around at work should happen several times during the day.

Moving is important to counteract the bad effects of our sedentary behavior and ensure that we expend all the energy we consume every day. But movement is about more than just expending energy: It is also about creating it. You know those times when you come back from a big workout and think, "Wow, I have so much energy!" It seems counterintuitive, but instead of feeling exhausted from working out, you actually feel like you have more energy, and you actually do have more energy. Here is why:

▶ *Our cells produce energy.* Exercise (like walking at a good pace on the treadmill or other forms of moderate to vigorous exercise) affects us at the cellular level, where energy production begins. Tiny organs called mitochondria, located in our cells, work like tiny power plants to produce energy. Much of the energy we need comes from our diet, which is why it is important to eat healthy food on a regular basis. But the number of mitochondria we have is affected by daily activity. The more cardiovascular exercise we perform, the more mitochondria our bodies make to produce more energy. Performing regular cardiovascular exercise actually creates more available energy for our bodies.

▶ *We consume more oxygen.* Any kind of physical exertion creates an increased need for oxygen. If we are not very physically fit, we may notice this need sooner than others, but at some point, we all find ourselves breathing heavier and faster during exercise. Because of this increased consumption of oxygen, our lung capacity also increases with exercise. Over time, aerobic capacity increases, allowing us to deliver more and more oxygen to our brains and bloodstream, helping us feel more awake, alert, and ready to go. In addition to allowing more oxygen to reach our brains and bloodstream, exercise allows our blood to circulate more efficiently, bringing more oxygen to our muscles and allowing for increased functioning throughout our bodies and heightened energy production.

▶ *Physical activity produces endorphins.* Endorphins are chemicals produced at the base of our brains that, when released, produce feelings of pain relief and well-being. In fact, the term *runner's high* refers to feelings of joy and excitement produced during strenuous physical activity because of the release of endorphins into the bloodstream. But even moderate or light physical activity causes our bodies to release endorphins, creating similar (if not as strong) effects on our mood. This lifting of our spirits and mood also creates the effect of making us feel more energized and ready to take on the rest of our day.

So why aren't we all like Catrine Tudor-Locke, taking every possible opportunity to jump on a treadmill and get in our steps? Why aren't we exercise fanatics just chomping at the bit to produce more energy? Well, it turns out *not* exercising regularly has the opposite effect on our bodies. Sitting all day, like so many of us do at work, leaves us lethargic and tired. Not the best motivator for moving or exercise.

EATING FOR ENERGY

When it comes to eating at work, the JJHPI concept of energy management is also a helpful framework. Elite athletes think of food as fuel—they have to, or they put themselves at risk of not performing their best, which directly impacts their career. If the rest of us all treated food and nutrition in the same way, we could see improvements in our performance as well. In order to maximize performance, it is critically important to keep our bodies fed with regular doses of good nutrition, but not to overeat. My nutritionist coach at JJHPI stressed the importance of eating every two to four hours, incorporating three meals and two to three "strategic snacks" every day. He suggested that meals should be about five "handfuls," or five rounded scoops of food, made up of a mix of proteins, grains, fruits, and vegetables. Snacks should be between 100 and 150 calories and low on the glycemic index—for example, Greek yogurt, a small handful of nuts, a large apple, or a tablespoon of peanut butter. The point is to eat enough to feel full and satisfied at meals, not stuffed, and to feel a little bit hungry right before snack time or mealtime. Eating "light and often" stabilizes glucose levels, improves metabolism, helps us maintain muscle mass, and improves energy levels, brain function, and mood.

Probably one of the biggest challenges for anyone today, but especially Americans, is portion control. Food is advertised everywhere and is always right at our fingertips! Our bodies are trained machines to eat what is available to us, and we do not know how to handle the draw of all of this incredible marketing on TV, on billboards, in restaurants, and in grocery stores. The problem (from an energy standpoint) is that when we give in to our cravings and overeat, it really messes with our blood sugar level. Eating too much causes us to have low energy and poor listening skills and be disengaged, fatigued, sluggish, and apathetic—all of which are not exactly conducive to getting work done. It can be difficult to focus on what our bodies are telling us we need versus what the external world is telling us we want. But our ability to listen to when we are full or hungry is an important skill for keeping our energy high all day.

LOSING WEIGHT AT WORK

Roughly 70 percent of Americans are overweight, and 70 percent of Americans' waking hours are spent at work during the week. It just makes sense to leverage work time and integrate healthy habits into our work style. But losing weight requires more than just getting in a good cardio workout. During my Corporate Athlete® training, my coaches spent a good deal of time focused on helping us understand weight loss. Most of the folks in my course were interested in losing a bit of weight, and many of us found our sedentary jobs a big part of the cause. We wanted to understand the science behind weight loss and start changing our behaviors at work. And most of us were interested in empowering our colleagues to do the same. I went into the course thinking that walking more during the day would solve all of our problems. I was wrong.

Our JJHPI exercise coach gave it to us straight: "If you want to lose weight, you have to commit to three strategies. The foundational strategy is good nutrition. You can't outwork a bad diet. The second most important strategy to losing weight is resistance training (two to three days a week) and then finally aerobic training (three to four days a week), specifically interval training." The good news about his advice, for all of us, is that all three of these strategies can be tackled during a workday, with some preparation. Here is a little more on resistance and interval training if you are not familiar with them.

Resistance Training

Resistance training, also known as strength training, is important because our muscle mass naturally diminishes with age. If we do not replace the lean muscle, we increase the percentage of fat in our bodies. As we gain muscle, our bodies begin to burn calories more efficiently, and the more toned our muscles, the easier it is to control weight. Many women have a difficult time with this concept because the media has done such a good job of associating strength training with bodybuilding. If you are a woman and feel this way, imagine a ballerina body, not someone with muscles like Arnold Schwarzenegger. Resistance movements do not have to be big. They can actually be really tiny, and repeated over and over, they can be highly effective and produce long, lean muscles. In addition to helping us lose or control weight, resistance training helps increase bone density, boost stamina, sharpen focus, and manage many chronic conditions including back pain, arthritis, obesity, heart disease, and diabetes.

There are many different ways to accomplish this kind of training. Most gyms have circuit training, where you rotate through weight machines, working out different muscles as you go. Other tools or techniques for resistance training include resistance bands, yoga, free weights, stability balls, BOSU and medicine balls, kettlebells, or your own body weight. Resistance training is ideal for doing at work because you can do it for 30 to 45 minutes at lunch or break it up into small chunks throughout your day. And most people do not sweat very much while doing it.

Interval Training

Remember that we still have bodies very similar to those of early humans, though our lifestyle has changed dramatically. There was actually a time when grocery stores did not exist and we had to hunt and scavenge for our food for survival. Often, we would have to survive for days and weeks without food before we found it again. It is actually surprising how long the human body can go without eating. At the age of 74, Mahatma Gandhi, the famous nonviolent campaigner for India's independence, survived 21 days of total starvation while allowing himself only sips of water. Other protesters on hunger strikes have survived as long as 40 days. My point here is not to encourage starvation, only to say that our bodies have an amazing ability to store fat and hold on to it very, very tightly for occasions when food might not be around. And our bodies will store as much fat as we let them store—which can be a lot! So convincing our bodies to hand over perfectly good "fat for a rainy day" takes some serious coaxing. That is where aerobic interval training comes into play.

Interval training involves a series of low- to high-intensity exercise bursts interspersed with rest or relief periods, repeated several times. These bursts can include walking (walking uphill or up stairs works great), running, cycling, rowing, swimming, using cardio machines, or using circuit machines. The idea with interval training is that we need to shock our bodies into using fat cells they desperately want to hold onto to keep us alive.

STRATEGIES TO INCREASE MOVEMENT AND EXERCISE AT WORK

Under Armour is a great American business success story and its logo is on many of the athletic clothing items in my closet. Founded in 1996, the company has an annual revenue of nearly $4 billion, with its products now available all over the world. The company is growing at a breakneck speed. I have spent a bit of time at their Baltimore global headquarters, interviewing leaders and employees and observing and analyzing the workplace.

One thing is abundantly clear: Their culture is pretty unique. Employees are called "teammates," and they frequently incorporate Under Armour clothing into their work wardrobes. There is a basketball court on campus for pick-up games and tournament play, and the health-conscious cafeteria is home to an enormous "living wall."

To say that the culture of this organization encourages exercise is an understatement. Though the employees work very hard, they are encouraged during the day to blow off steam and go for a run, shoot some hoops, or do yoga on the promenade overlooking the city. (See Figure 4-1.) They are even allowed to test their own clothing and equipment for research purposes. The culture and the physical environment at the company, obviously supported by the leadership and brand, are all about human performance and getting things done with the health of Under Armour employees (and customers) in mind. What is abundantly clear to me about the Under Armour campus, from talking to some of the company's leaders and seeing how employees work, is that the campus is full of movement and energy. Under Armour is a testament that there are several ways to increase movement and energy during the workday, and to integrate it into work life, even for those whose job is more sedentary.

The Under Armour Performance Center (the on-campus gym) is powered by FX Studios, a fitness company based in Baltimore, which first partnered with Under Armour in 2010 to design and manage the fitness facilities. The majority of gym members are Under Armour employees, but community members are also welcome to join. Employees are provided with a monthly stipend for training at the gym, whether they are a member or not, and this has encouraged more employees to try out sessions and eventually become hooked. All training sessions (typically with fewer than eight people) and classes are led by personal trainers with extensive experience. These group sessions have been a great way for employees

Figure 4-1. Under Armour yoga class on the company's Tide Point campus in Baltimore. Image courtesy of Under Armour Performance Center powered by FX Fitness.

across the organization to get to know each other. The relationships they make during training are important for building relationships to help the business. Want to spend more quality time with your boss? Go for a run with him or her around the campus! Want to improve the effectiveness of your team? Try weekly workouts together! The large number of classes throughout the day or evening makes this easy (40 different classes are offered each week). According to Nate Costa, CEO of FX Studios, "Being active is encouraged at Under Armour. We feel it's important to challenge your body and your mind." [4]

Classes for individuals of all fitness levels are available. The trainers on campus have found that when they offer the same class over and over again, exercises get easier and less exciting. "There are a thousand ways to work each muscle in your body. Our challenge is to create programs that challenge our workforce," said Costa. The UA Well team, focused on improving the health of Under Armour teammates, has found that competition is also a highly effective tool, often more so than monetary incentives. For example, Under Armour has more than 300 retail stores globally, and each store acts as a workout team. Trainers at the Under Amour Performance Center send out different exercise reps for store employees to do for a few minutes each day to rack up points for their team. Competitions are held to help tie retail employees to those at headquarters, and the majority of retail stores participate in these challenges.

Under Armour has recently acquired several fitness applications and integrated them into the Under Armour Connected Fitness™ platform, which now holds the world's largest digital health and fitness community through a suite of apps including UA Record, MapMyFitness, Endomondo, and MyFitnessPal. Many employees use apps on the platform to store their activities, and Under Armour's personal trainers use the data to customize workouts during training sessions.

The key with integrating movement successfully into the workplace—even at a place with a culture as active as Under Armour—is to use interventions that actually work. Those that have been shown to be most effective are typically a combination of strategies, including information (prompts or community-wide campaigns), behavioral and social interventions (social support or individually adapted health behavior strategies), and environment and policy interventions (providing a place for physical activity combined with informational outreach activities).[5] In other words, workers need to be given some combination of knowledge, support, training, a place, and permission to move around at work. Here are some strategies to encourage your employees (especially those who are more sedentary and need it) to move and exercise more.

■ Use "Point of Decision" Prompts

Studies show that by just letting people know the health benefits of taking the stairs and showing their location (like putting a sign in the elevator lobby or using stair riser banners), stair usage increases by 54 percent![6] But think beyond just a little sign: There is a significant amount of wall space in most workplaces. Many organizations use their walls to integrate community-wide campaigns throughout the workplace to share best practices in movement, exercise, nutrition, sleep, and how these practices help boost energy levels. At Under Armour, many of the walls are used to display images and videos of highly attractive athletes wearing the company's clothing products and showing off their abilities. The company is (subliminally) marketing health to its employees as well as customers.

As another example, New York City launched a big movement campaign to encourage taking the stairs using neon green posters and a catchy slogan, "Burn Calories, Not Electricity. Take the Stairs!" As of 2014, 30,000 stair prompts had been distributed in more than 1,000 buildings.[7] Another one of my favorite prompts is a sign with a bike and a car. By the bike it says "Eats fat and gives you energy." By the car it says "Eats energy and makes you fat."

65

▪ Make Stairs More Attractive to Use

Taking the stairs is good for lowering cholesterol levels, for burning calories, and for encouraging employees to bump into each other and collaborate.[8] However, getting people to take the stairs can sometimes require more than clever signage. In modern building design, the elevator is front and center and stairways are often hidden, dark, locked (for fire code purposes), and generally scary places to hang out. Not exactly ideal for encouraging health. So if it's possible to choose a building or to design your space with an open, airy stair—one with daylight, views, artwork, or nice finishes—it will increase the chances of it being used. (See an example in Figure 4-2.) If your local building code allows, use a magnetic "hold open" on the stair door (which releases in the case of a fire). You can also change your building elevator settings to "skip stops," so that the elevators stop only every other floor or every three floors, which encourages people to take at least one flight of stairs. At Arbor House, a low-income rental apartment in the South Bronx in New York City, the stairs play nice music and the elevators are silent. Also, elevators in the building are programmed to intentionally be very slow, which naturally encourages more stair use.[9]

▪ Encourage Employees to Stand Up

Standing is good for us even though we are not moving. It does not compensate for exercise, but it activates our large leg muscles, which is good for cardio metabolic health.[10] Encourage employees to take phone calls, watch presentations, read, or perform other activities while standing up if they typically work

Figure 4-2. Haberlin Hall, Chemistry & Physics building study space, the College of the Holy Cross, Worcester, Massachusetts, designed by EYP. Image courtesy of EYP, ©Robert Benson Photography.

sitting down all day. More and more organizations are providing their employees with sit-to-stand desks (adjustable desks that can be easily moved to accommodate sitting or standing workers), but even if this is not an immediate option, consider providing some work points at standing height in the workspace so that employees can stand and work from time to time. Many leaders host stand-up meetings as well, which are typically shorter and more focused than traditional meetings as well as a great way to increase energy. Standing meetings model good behavior, which is often required to make people feel they have "permission" to work a little differently.

Standing meetings can also boost creativity and engagement. Researchers at Washington University in St. Louis did a study to understand how group creativity and engagement might increase or decrease based on changes to the physical environment. They split student subjects into two groups, both of which were put in a conference room and asked to come up with a short promotional video for their school in 30 minutes. The first group did this exercise sitting around a conference table, while the second group had no chairs and did the exercise standing up. The researchers found differences in the creativity and execution of the videos between the two groups, but also in the social dynamics in the room. Individuals in the standing group were more engaged and more likely to toss out their own ideas and pick up on a better one from someone else, and there was less group hierarchy in the room. As a result, the quality of the videos was much higher than that of the group that sat around the table. The simple change of removing furniture and allowing teams to work more dynamically in the room dramatically changed the creative output.[11]

▪ Encourage and Enable Employees to Walk

Clearly, walking regularly during the day is a good thing for employee health, creativity, and engagement, and walking meetings are starting to become all the rage in business. The idea has actually been around for a while. Aristotle, Sigmund Freud, Harry Truman, Charles Dickens, Steve Jobs, and now Facebook's Mark Zuckerberg and Twitter's Jack Dorsey have all been known to favor walking meetings. Walking meetings (compared to meetings sitting around a table) tend to be much more natural and focused on the topics at hand. According to neuroscientist Andrew Tate, the increased blood flow to your brain "helps you express those ideas more fluently and helps you communicate with coworkers."[12] If your organization is moving into a new space or has the opportunity to renovate, consider slightly wider hallways, more attractive and efficient staircases, and treadmill desks.

■ Locate Your Office Space by Public Transportation or Amenities

Building location and good urban planning can impact people movement. For example, research shows that proximity to parks and other recreational facilities is consistently associated with higher levels of physical activity and healthier weight status among youth and adults.[13] The same goes for proximity to public transit: There is a link between access to public transportation and physical activity, since transit use typically involves walking to and from a bus or subway stop. In one study, compared to car commuters, train commuters walked an average of 30 percent more steps per day and were four times more likely to walk 10,000 steps per day.[14] Many organizations encourage employees to use public transportation for environmental reasons, but it turns out there are excellent health benefits as well.

■ Provide a Place for Employees to Work Out

If you have the space and budget for it, nothing beats having a gym either in the building, on campus, or just a few blocks from the office. The closer to where employees work, the better. If your company has the budget or space for a gym, consider providing gym memberships for free or at a greatly reduced price. Especially if the workplace is in a very cold or very hot climate, there are significant portions of the year when it is practically impossible to exercise outside, and an indoor workout environment is essential. Ideally, exercise rooms should have nice windows as research shows that exercise is more appealing when it occurs in spaces with views to nature and human activities.[15] (For an example, see Figure 4-3.) Warm colors, especially when accompanied by high illumination levels, have also been found to encourage activity or movement, whereas cool colors promote more passive behavior.[16]

Figure 4-3. Workout facility with views to nature, Connecticut College, New London, Connecticut. Image courtesy of EYP, © Jim Fiora Studio.

▪ Double Up Workspace for Exercise or Stretching

My team has observed more than 6,000 conference rooms globally over the last three years. We know that most conference rooms are used only 25 percent of the time, and larger rooms even less than that. This is because 75 percent of meetings today involve only two to four people.[17] (The complaints we hear about "not being able to find a conference room" are typically the result of ineffective reservation protocols—for example, groups signing up for a room and then not showing up.) So reserve one of these larger conference rooms at nonpeak meeting times (avoid Mondays through Thursdays from 10 a.m. to 2 p.m., when most large meetings occur), and turn your meeting space into a workout room for yoga, tai chi, Pilates, or other workout programs of your choice. A surprising number of exercises can be done in space you already have.

I recently spoke with a manager from a pharmaceutical organization in New Zealand who decided to take a conference room on his floor "out of service" and put in 20 spinning bikes instead. He even agreed to lead a spin class, even though he had never taught one before. At first, everyone thought he was nuts, but after a few months, people caught on and started spinning in the room on a regular basis. This manager claims it really livened up the physical environment and transformed the way the team worked and collaborated for the better. At The Motley Fool, a midsize investment services and advisory firm based in Alexandria, Virginia, the company recently started holding what it calls "active meetings," where employees are encouraged to exercise in the middle of business meetings. Regardless of whether anyone else finds it distracting, employees get down on the floor and do push-ups in the middle of a meeting, or a leader might order everyone to get into a sitting position against the wall to strengthen their legs.[18]

■ Carve Out Space for Bikes and Showers

If your office has people who like to bike, skate, or scoot to work, create a small space in the building for their storage. Some companies have gotten creative and celebrate their biker community. At HOK's Atlanta office, employees' commuter bikes have become art and a great conversation piece. (See Figure 4-4.) Google offices are full of "scooter parking," in support of movement throughout the buildings.

STRATEGIES TO IMPROVE NUTRITION AT WORK

When it comes to influencing better eating choices at work, most organizations provide education about what foods to eat and/or change the worksite environment in some way. Environmental changes might include nutrition policies and practices such as nutrition labeling, vending policies, cafeteria food supply/availability, and menu reformulation. Research is weak on the health outcomes of these changes because most of the studies out there involve self-reporting, which can be suspect. (I mean, how can we expect people to be honest about what they eat? I can barely remember what I ate yesterday!) That said, the evidence suggests that economic incentives can positively impact dietary behavior as well as changing the "rules" or policies as to what is socially acceptable to eat at work.[19] Here are some effective strategies to encourage your employees to eat healthier (and create more energy).

■ Provide a Place for Employees to Eat and to Store
  Their Lunch

Americans eat in a restaurant five times a week, according to a survey conducted by LivingSocial. The survey, with 4,000 respondents, identified lunch as the most popular meal to eat

Figure 4-4. Bicycle storage at HOK's Atlanta office. Image courtesy of HOK, Mai&Bri Photography, maibri.com.

out. Lunch meals eaten outside the workplace, both carryout and sit-down, averaged 2.6 per week.[20]

By bringing in their own snacks and lunch and not eating out, employees automatically make better choices because they are more aware of what they are putting in their mouth. Encouraging employees to provide their own lunch and giving them a nice place to store and eat it makes it easier for them to make healthier food choices. Eating spaces should have access to natural light and views and should be generally pleasant and convenient—not shoved in a space in the basement or a closet somewhere. They can also be used for functions besides eating if designed well. (See Figure 4-5 for an example of a good multipurpose eating space.)

Figure 4-5. Multipurpose eating area at EYP Architecture & Engineering, Boston office. Photo credit: Richard Mandelkorn Photography.

Provide Healthy, Portioned Meals or Snacks for Employees

When it comes to food, a good offense is the best defense. A surprising number of companies are providing or subsidizing healthy food at the workplace for breakfast, lunch, dinner, and/or snacks. The reasons for this vary. It might be because the company sees this strategy as a benefit, a recruiting/retention tool, a way to keep employees on-site, or possibly because there are no other food choices in the neighborhood and the worksite is in a "food desert." Whatever the case, putting food into the right-size portions for a healthy meal (and not supersized) can make it easier for employees to eat only when they are hungry.

Make Healthy Choices the Default Setting

You know how you walk into a grocery store and find yourself buying food you find at the end of the aisle? Or why candy is located at child-eye level by the checkout counter? Foods that are easy to spot and presented well are not put there by accident, and food companies pay for the privilege. The secret is *choice architecture,* a term for different ways in which choices can be presented to consumers, and the impact of that presentation on consumer decision making. For example, the number of choices presented, the manner in which attributes are described, and the presence of a "default" can all influence consumer choice. Many companies are using this strategy by reducing the number of unhealthy foods in the workplace or by making them harder to find.

Nutritionists recommend putting healthy food in glass containers and placing them prominently on a table or in the refrigerator. Studies have shown that people are much more likely to eat food found in a glass container over food in something you can't see through. Google has implemented this strategy in many of its break areas by storing candy in opaque containers and displaying healthier snacks, such as pistachios, in glass jars. The company also has started putting its own nutrition labels on foods so that Googlers are highly aware of the food choices they are making.[21] Some companies also use glass doors on their refrigerators to remind employees of the healthy food options inside (versus processed snacks that might be more visible because they do not require refrigeration).

Brian Wansink, director of Cornell University's Food and Brand Lab and author of *Mindless Eating*, suggests a number of ways our eating behavior is significantly impacted by the way food is presented to us. For example, in some of his studies, people were likely to snack less (44 percent less) in kitchens that were tidy versus kitchens that were cluttered with paper, dirty dishes, etc. So keeping the kitchen clean is more than just a sanitation issue—it can affect how much we eat! In another study, Wansink found that people were more likely to eat less on plates that are 9–10 inches in diameter. People tended to pile up food on plates that were larger than that, and they felt "deprived" and went for a second helping when they had smaller plates (say, 6 inches in diameter). Other studies of his show that people are likely to serve themselves 20 percent less food on plates with contrasting colors to the food they are eating, such as white pasta on a red or blue plate.[22]

Many companies are using choice architecture because it is effective, but it is also important for organizations to continue to provide food choices to suit a variety of tastes. People love diversity in their diet just as they always have for generations. If companies get too draconian with what foods they provide to employees, it can feel coercive and not have the desired effect. The best way to go about this is to have a licensed dietician survey your population and make recommendations on what foods to provide, as well as how to prepare and display them.

◾ Leverage Healthy Catering and Vending Options

Changing the way your company works with its food vendors involves procurement, new contract terms, and employee buy-in and can be fraught with resistance. But given that employees spend 8, 12, and sometimes 16 hours in the workplace every day, providing access to inexpensive, healthy food and making it easy to find has a major impact on their health. Several organizations have written contracts with vendors that explicitly call for vendors to provision, place, package, and label food in a way to encourage healthy choices. The good news is that healthy food, vending, and snack companies are, in general, becoming more popular. For example, companies like HUMAN Healthy Vending and Fresh Healthy Vending provide healthy food and drinks in vending machines, and companies like WorkPerks send your office a variety of healthy office snacks in a nice wooden box for your pantry or kitchen area. One large company I interviewed has an online catering service that provides healthy choices for meetings, including a "celebration guide" that offers smaller portions of sweets to use when celebrating employee birthdays, work anniversaries, or retirements.

◾ Provide Places for Employees to Grow Their Own Food

Urban agriculture, vertical farms, and community gardens are starting to really take on more importance as our cities get more congested. Depending on the constraints of your workspace, providing employees the opportunity to grow and harvest their own fruits, vegetables, and herbs could be a wonderful opportunity to encourage healthy eating, as well as creating a sense of community. Recent studies show that people are more likely to eat more healthy foods if they have a hand in growing their own food as a community, and even more so than if they grow it on their own![23] Even if employees can't grow food themselves, there may be opportunities to use your workplace as a teaching tool for growing and eating healthy foods. As an example, Eskenazi Health in Indianapolis has partnered with Growing Places Indy to operate a sky farm at the new Sidney & Lois Eskenazi Hospital and Eskenazi Health campus. The 5,000-square-foot Sky Farm is open to patients, staff, and the community as a space to engage with food and learn how it grows, how to prepare fresh produce, and why it's important to health. Items grown at the Sky Farm are also made available to patients, visitors, and staff.[24]

So your employees are eating well, exercising . . . all is good, right? Well, it turns out that creating energy is a foundation for productivity, but there are other critical aspects to health that affect our emotions and spirit and that can also impact performance—maybe more than you think. Owens Corning, a global manufacturer of roofing, insulation, and fiberglass composites, has about 15,000 employees in 26 countries. The company recently surveyed a sampling of its population in partnership with Harvard's School of Public Health and asked employees, "How many days did your physical or mental health keep you from doing your usual activities over the last 30 days?" They calculated a loss of 3,513 days over the last month due to presenteeism and absenteeism—equivalent to 5 percent of the workforce. Interestingly, employees believed they lost productivity due to mental health issues twice as often as from physical health problems.[25]

So how are companies getting a handle on mental health, stress, and other sometimes "stealth" issues impacting the inner work-life of their employees? And can they back up claims that improving mental health improves the bottom line? It turns out, they can.

5

Reduce Stress, Increase Focus

WENT ROCK CLIMBING FOR THE first time recently. I consider myself a fairly athletic person, but this activity definitely took me out of my comfort zone. Despite being "on belay," or harnessed, and in the hands of an expert on the ground below, I got about 75 percent up a 50-foot climbing wall and just froze. I was out of breath, mentally and physically taxed, a little freaked out, and I could not figure out how to get any further up the wall. My arms and legs just could not reach any more of those tiny colored knobs. At this point, having no other options, I stopped for a minute on a rock crevice, took some giant yoga breaths, and looked around at the beautiful scenery around me. I was surrounded by the Sonoran Desert—full of cactus plants and the Santa Catalina Mountains. The quiet of nature sunk in and I thought about the spectacular view. Then, amazingly, after about a minute of focused breathing, I found the mental and physical strength to figure out a new climbing route and make it to the top. For me, this was a great lesson in "taking a breather when things get tough." Now, when work gets stressful—and it can get really stressful sometimes—I take a few deep yoga breaths and look outside or maybe take a short walk. I learned later that this deep breathing produces what's called a relaxation response in the body that is important for getting your brain to focus on being productive, not stay in permanent "fight, flight, or freeze" mode.

Most of the time, stress is talked about as a negative thing, but the truth is that not all stress is bad. All animals have a stress response, which can be lifesaving in some situations. The nerve chemicals and hormones released during such stressful times prepare animals like us to face a threat or flee to safety. When we face a dangerous situation, our pulse quickens, we breathe faster, our muscles tense, and our brains use more oxygen and increase activity—all functions aimed at survival. In the short term, stress can even boost our immune system.

Problems occur if the stress response goes on too long, such as when the source of stress is constant, or if the response continues after the danger has subsided. Over time, continued strain on our bodies from routine stress can lead to serious health problems, such as anxiety disorder, depression, digestive issues, heart disease, sleep problems, weight gain, and memory and concentration impairment.

The thing about stress that is really counterproductive for the workplace is that it shuts down our ability to be creative and to make calm, thoughtful decisions. When we are stressed, we get very reactive and tense. Have you ever been really stressed out at the office—with your phone ringing off the hook while you are simultaneously responding to seven emails and you have someone waiting for something standing by your desk—and you thought, "Wow, I just had a brilliant insight and I'm going to reflect on that for a minute"? No, this probably did not happen, because when we encounter a perceived threat—our boss yells at us or we are under a deadline, for instance—our hypothalamus, a tiny region at the base of the brain, sets off an alarm system in the body. Through a combination of nerve and hormonal signals, this system prompts our adrenal glands, located by the kidneys, to release a surge of hormones, including adrenaline and cortisol. Adrenaline increases heart rate, elevates blood pressure, and boosts energy supplies. Cortisol, the primary stress hormone, increases sugars (glucose) in the bloodstream, enhances the brain's use of glucose, and increases the availability of substances that repair tissues. Cortisol also curbs functions that would be nonessential or detrimental in a fight-or-flight situation. It alters immune system responses and suppresses the digestive system, the reproductive system, and growth processes. This complex natural alarm system also communicates with regions of the brain that control mood, motivation, and fear.

Making calm, thoughtful decisions when we are stressed out is just about physically impossible. Fortunately, there are many ways to calm down and reverse the crazy hormonal party happening in our bodies. The key to stress is to understand how it affects us physiologically and then manage it in a productive way.

WORKPLACE STRESSORS

Managing stress at work and helping to keep it under control is important for both our health and our success at work. Without a strategy in place for managing stress, we are likely not our most productive, professional selves. Plus, the stress of our job affects not only our performance at work but how we behave outside work and, as a result, it can impact our family and friends. As Sharon Salzberg, a Buddhist meditation teacher and writer, says, "It's hard to give from a source of depletion."[1] More than half of Americans say they fight with friends and loved ones because of stress, and more than 70 percent say they experience real physical and emotional symptoms from it.[2] Here are some indicators that we need to de-stress:

82

▶ We are less patient and sympathetic listening to other people's problems.

▶ We ask more closed-end questions to discourage dialogue.

▶ Our dedication to exercise, diet, and friendship wanes.

▶ We feel trapped.

▶ We give people a lot of "Yes, but . . . " answers to suggestions.

▶ We have lost our sense of humor.

So what is causing us to behave this way at work? The list of reasons is long! It could be having a bad commute, having a disagreement with a colleague or boss, dealing with a personnel issue, having crazy deadlines, being afraid of being fired, addressing a life-threatening situation (if you are in the military, a firefighter, etc.), taking on too much responsibility, working long hours, or having no control over the outcomes of your work.

Then there are "stealth stressors" like email, texts, or instant messages. Back in the old days, if we had received as much snail mail as the average American receives in electronic mail today, our office would be filled with paper after about a day. Email can be really overwhelming, but getting electronic messages and texts is like crack cocaine. We feel this incredible urge to check messages at all times. I am totally addicted to the little buzz my phone gives me when I receive a message. It is like someone just sent me a little present, only it is not really a gift at all. Typically, when I get emails for work (or texts or voicemails or instant messages), it is *not* because people want to thank me for being such an awesome person and making the world a better place. They are sending me a message because they want me to do something for them, usually something I was not planning to do at all until I read their message. Now that I have read the message and know what they want me to do, I have to decide if I should do it now or later.

About 19 percent of corporate email is junk mail (according to a study by the Radicati Group), but the remaining emails are legitimate requests for our attention.[3] Sherry Turkle's *Alone Together* gives a frightening account of how technology has taken over our lives and our ability to communicate, and it provides countless ways technology causes stress. She writes: "Anxiety is part of the new connectivity. Yet, it is often the missing term when we talk about the revolution in mobile communications."[4]

So how do we get control of stressors at work? How can we make our lives saner and keep some perspective every day? And what steps can employers take to ensure that employee stress is minimized and productivity is maximized?

THE BENEFITS OF MINDFULNESS

There are fundamental ways to combat stress, like sleeping, getting regular exercise, and eating well. But there are also some specific techniques we can apply to stressful situations as they occur throughout the day. One common method is referred to as the *relaxation response*, coined by Dr. Herbert Benson, a cardiologist and founder of Harvard's Mind Body Medical Institute (now called the Benson-Henry Institute for Mind Body Medicine). Benson describes this response as the ability to encourage the body to release chemicals and brain signals that make our muscles and organs slow down and increase blood flow to the brain—the reverse of the fight-or-flight response. Benson has seen, as have many of his colleagues in the medical profession, that regular practice of the relaxation response can be an effective treatment for a wide range of stress-related disorders.[5] There are several methods to elicit the relaxation response, including visualization, progressive muscle relaxation, energy healing, acupuncture, massage, breathing techniques, prayer, meditation, tai chi, qigong, yoga, and meditation.

Before we get into the many ways companies have tapped into strategies that trigger the relaxation response to reduce stress and increase the productivity and creativity of their employees, it is worth giving a quick overview of meditation in particular. There is a great deal of science and emerging research behind the benefits of meditation, particularly *mindfulness meditation*, which has captured the attention of business leaders, members of the U.S. Congress, military commanders, hospital administrators, and pro sports coaches.

Mindfulness meditation specifically focuses on concentration and "open awareness," or being objectively aware of what we are thinking and feeling. Mindfulness is found in many contemplative traditions, but it is most often identified with the Theravada Buddhist practice of vipassana, or "insight meditation." This mindfulness practice is often extended to daily actions, such as eating, walking, driving, or routine tasks. It was originally brought to practice in the Western world around 30 years ago and made popular by Eckhart Tolle (a German-born Canadian who has written extensively on the subject), Jon Kabat-Zinn, and others. Kabat-Zinn, an MIT-trained molecular biologist, was a student of Buddhist teachers such as Thich Nhat Hanh and Zen master Seung Sahn, and his practice of yoga and studies with Buddhist teachers led him to integrate their teachings with those of Western science. He created a process called mindfulness-based stress reduction (MBSR), now commonly offered by medical centers, hospitals, and health insurance organizations.

The essence of MBSR and other related meditation techniques is to help us focus on the present, rather than the past or the future. As humans, we have an incredible gift and a curse at the same time: We are self-aware. We can observe our own thoughts, talk to ourselves, perceive how others perceive us, and generally stress ourselves out. How exactly? By focusing enormous amounts of time on brooding about the past and obsessing over the future, and spending no time enjoying and taking in the "present," or observing and responding to what is actually happening to us. To quote Dan Harris—an ABC news anchor, meditator, and author of *10% Happier*—"We live our lives in a fog of projection and rumination."[6]

Meditation requires that we "work out" our brain muscles in a different way. Instead of trying to think about 10 things at once, which is normal for most people, when we meditate we are required to focus on only one thing at a time and with full concentration, like focusing on just our breathing. This focused practice gives our brains the muscles they need to focus attention and *respond, not react* to events as they unfold in our lives. It also helps us keep our minds from wandering quite so much, which tends to happen about 47 percent of our waking hours, according to a study by psychologists Matthew A. Killingsworth, a Robert Wood Johnson Foundation Health & Society Scholar, and Daniel T. Gilbert of Harvard University. They have found that: "Unlike other animals, humans spend a lot of time thinking about what isn't going on around them: contemplating events that happened in the past, might happen in the future, or may never happen at all. Indeed, mind-wandering appears to be the human brain's default mode of operation."[7]

Other researchers did a study scanning the brains of people who were "meditation novices." After an eight-week MBSR course, participants reported reductions in stress but also were found to have a reduction of gray-matter density in the part of the brain called the amygdala, which is known to play an important role in anxiety and stress. So the area in the brain that "stresses out" literally shrank in these subjects after just eight weeks of meditating for the first time. Also, *increased* gray-matter density appeared in their hippocampus, known to be important for learning and memory, and in structures associated with self-awareness, compassion, and introspection.[8] These people became smarter, more thoughtful, and nicer because they meditated. And as compelling as this study is, it is just one of many that are hitting medical journals every day, laying out the personal and business benefits of spending just a few minutes calming and focusing the mind every day. The Mayo Clinic claims meditators gain a new perspective on stressful situations, build skills to manage stress, increase self-awareness, focus on the present, and reduce negative emotions. Studies are also under way that potentially link meditation to helping people manage conditions such as anxiety disorders, asthma, cancer, depression, heart disease, high blood pressure, pain, and even sleep problems.[9]

Is your company interested in creating a meditation initiative? According to Joy Rains, a meditation speaker and author who works with organizations to develop their meditation programs, the thing about meditation is that it requires space and time, which take some planning for, especially at work.[10]

■ Meditation Space

Many offices have meditation or health and wellness rooms that can be used for this purpose. For example, the World Bank has meditation rooms specifically designed for staff to decompress. But workplaces also may have other features that can support a meditative practice without necessarily dedicating space to it. Conference rooms, especially those out of high-traffic areas, work really well for seated meditation. My office in Washington, DC, happens to be located near a park with a labyrinth, which is perfect for a walking meditation. The U.S. Food and Drug Administration buildings in College Park, Maryland, have little percussion instrument sounds that beat under a covered walkway between the parking lot and the front of the building, a feature that was not originally designed for meditation but can serve as a focal point for a short sound meditation. Your workplace may have natural or even synthetic elements that can serve to pull your mind away from the stress of the day and focus on something else to give it release. The most important requirement for an effective meditation space is that it feels "safe" and free from distraction.

■ Time for Meditation

Meditation is a helpful stress reduction technique at work anytime, but according to Rains, the ideal time to meditate is before you or your team get too involved in the workday. The purpose of meditation is to increase awareness.[11] In the early morning hours, you are more aware of what you are feeling as opposed to at the end of the day, when you may be too tired to concentrate. Another good time to meditate is after doing some sort of physical activity. Once you have burned off physical energy, it is easier to quiet the mind, especially if you are new to the practice. If you have ever taken a yoga class, you notice that the sequence of the class generally involves moving at the beginning of the session and a meditation practice at the end for this very reason. Interestingly, many yoga practices are purely designed for "stretching out" and preparing the body so that you can sit and meditate for long periods of time without being fidgety.

MINDFULNESS AND BUSINESS

Many leaders and organizations over the years have tapped into mindfulness meditation or other forms of deep individual reflection to gain a competitive advantage, but you might be surprised that some of the most impactful examples have come from sports and the military.

> ► *Basketball.* Widely considered one of the greatest coaches in the history of the NBA, Phil Jackson was the head coach of the Chicago Bulls from 1989 until 1998, during which time Chicago won six NBA championships. His

next team, the Los Angeles Lakers, won five champion-ships with Jackson as head coach. Jackson attributes all this success to a holistic approach to coaching that is influenced by Eastern philosophy, earning him the nickname "Zen Master." He cites Robert Pirsig's book *Zen and the Art of Motorcycle Maintenance* as one of the major guiding forces in his life. "Awareness is every-thing," Jackson wrote in his book *Sacred Hoops.* "The se-cret is not thinking. That doesn't mean being stupid. It means quieting the endless jabbering of thoughts so that your body can do instinctively what it's been trained to do without the mind getting in the way."[12]

▶ *Football.* Pete Carroll, head coach of the Seattle Seahawks NFL team, claims that high performance is "all about clearing the clutter in the interactions between your conscious and subconscious mind." He has used these techniques to get his team to the Super Bowl in 2014 and 2015. Seahawks quarterback Russell Wilson has been working with a mental conditioning consultant, Trevor Moawad, since preparing for the NFL draft in 2012, to help maintain heightened levels of awareness, focus, and leadership. Other members of the Seahawks work with Michael Gervais, a high-performance psy-chologist. Gervais claims, "What I've learned from the greatest athletes in the world is that the importance of being 'aware' is paramount. It really seems as though those who can live in the present moment, whatever the conditions that might be around them . . . that's [a strategy] for all of us."[13]

▶ *The Navy.* Former Navy Commander Mark Divine re-veals exercises, meditations, and focusing techniques to train the mind for mental toughness, emotional resil-ience, and intuition in his book *The Way of the Seal: Think Like an Elite Warrior to Lead and Succeed.*

▶ *The Marines.* Marine Corps officials are now testing a series of brain calming exercises called Mindfulness-based Mind Fitness Training (MMFT) that they believe will enhance the performance of troops, who are under mounting pressures from long deployments. Initial results of studies on the technique from the *American Journal of Psychiatry* indicate that Marines who received MMFT showed more mental resilience and recovered better than those that did not.[14]

Examples from sports and the military are particularly compelling when it comes to mindfulness because we can imagine the stress that individuals on the court, on the ball field, or on the battlefield have to endure and the benefits of relieving this stress under pressure. It is also easy to see how "mission-centered" tasks would benefit from focus—to help athletes or warriors concentrate on the important task at hand, either winning a game or fulfilling a military mission. But can mindfulness help people in different kinds of jobs, like investment bankers, teachers, accountants, or doctors? The business world is just beginning the journey to mindfulness and only now starting to witness the incredible abilities of mindful behavior and thinking in the workplace. But there are a growing number of examples of how meditation has helped people in many work settings accomplish great individual and team success.

I recently attended a conference in New York, called Wisdom 2.0 Business, that opened my eyes to the possibilities. The conference, which started on the West Coast in 2010 and has quickly expanded across the country, is the brainchild of founder Soren Gordhamer, who felt it was important to talk about one of the great challenges of our age: to live connected to one another through technology, and to bring awareness, compassion, and consciousness to our interactions to better ourselves and our world. The conference in New York included a mix of leaders representing large and small businesses, all of which believe that being more mindful, practicing meditation or yoga, or just leaving space in their lives for reflection was key to their personal and business success.

During the conference, each panel began with a meditation or a mental break, which really helped with concentration over the course of an intense day and a half sitting in a relatively dark room. Attendees came from across the world and from a surprising number of industries, all looking for ways to reduce stress and increase their engagement and happiness in a more methodical way. Also attending were a large number of small business owners who wanted to jump-start their "mindful-related" businesses, such as meditation or yoga instructors, executive coaches, or socially aware companies. I felt certain a conference like this never would have existed even just a few years ago, but it was clear that the concept is not only here to stay but growing.

It's fair to say that mindfulness, meditation, yoga, and other stress reduction techniques, at least in the United States, have really taken root in technology companies on the West Coast. Google, Apple, Facebook, LinkedIn, Intel, eBay, and Twitter are all creating stress reduction programs, and these days, companies almost *have* to do so in order to compete for top talent in their industry. What is fascinating about the mindfulness movement, though, is that it is now being adopted and championed outside the tech industry and across all regions of the United States and many parts of the world. Here are some tech and non-tech companies that are trying it and the results they are seeing.

■ Google

Bill Duane, formerly an engineer at Google and now superintendent of well-being and sustainable performance learning there, started a beginner's meditation class called "Self-Neural Hacking" at Google several years ago. It quickly became a full-scale meditation and mindfulness program for the company. According to Duane, he "used to use burgers and bourbon" to help with stress, but he long ago found that meditation works much better. Google's "Search Inside Yourself" leadership program, pioneered by Chade-Meng Tan (an early Google employee), has introduced mindfulness to more than 5,000 Googlers and 5,000 people working for companies outside Google. In typical Google fashion, Tan has turned their stress reduction program into a new business venture! The program is scientifically based yet practical, appealing to engineers but also to business leaders who are looking for strategies and techniques for increasing mindfulness without a lot of cultural or religious overtones. Googlers see the key benefits of the program as increasing emotional intelligence (understanding individual motivations), resilience in stressful situations, and focus—all critical skills for success in their business.

Apple

Meditation has long been promoted at Apple, initially because Steve Jobs benefited from it personally and saw the incredible benefits to business and innovation in his company. Employees at Apple can take up to 30 minutes each day to meditate at work, and the company provides classes on meditation and yoga on-site, offering the use of a meditation room. Providing these benefits is not just continuing Jobs's legacy. The company sees it as a competitive advantage and a benefit required to keep employees' creative juices flowing. Jobs told his biographer, Walter Isaacson:

> If you just sit and observe, you will see how restless your mind is. If you try to calm it, it only makes it worse, but over time it does calm, and when it does, there's room to hear more subtle things—that's when your intuition starts to blossom and you start to see things more clearly and be

in the present more. Your mind just slows down, and you see a tremendous expanse in the moment. You see so much more than you could see before. It's a discipline; you have to practice it.[15]

■ Aetna

Mark Bertolini is the CEO of Aetna, a diversified health care benefits company based in Hartford, Connecticut. Several years ago, he was in a severe skiing accident that gave him a serious spinal cord injury and left him partially disabled. The injury prompted him to investigate alternative healing methods such as acupuncture, meditation, and yoga. Bertolini still suffers from spinal cord pain but believes that practicing meditation and yoga each morning makes his pain manageable, as well as helping him keep focus during very busy days. His is a beneficiary of mindful ways to manage pain and stress, and he has encouraged and enabled employees at Aetna to benefit from them too—and with a good business case behind him.

Aetna determined in 2010 that each of its workers with the highest levels of stress were costing the company $2000 more each year than their coworkers. So the company kicked off a 12-week pilot with California- and Connecticut-based employees. *Human Resources Executive Magazine* reports:

> The outside researchers who assisted in the pilot randomized 239 employee volunteers into a therapeutic yoga worksite-stress-reduction program, one of two mindfulness-based programs, or into a control group that participated only in an assessment. Compared with the control group, the mind-body interventions showed statistically significant greater improvements on participants' perceived stress and sleep difficulties. Both the mindfulness and yoga interventions demonstrated significant improvements in heart-rhythm coherence, which is

a measure of how the body handles stress. The researchers concluded that both mindfulness-based and therapeutic yoga programs might be effective interventions to
target employees' high stress levels, sleep quality and
stress response.[16]

In 2012, the program helped reduce employee health benefit costs by 7 percent. According to David Gelles, a *New York
Times* reporter and author of *Mindful Work*:

> More than one-quarter of [Aetna]'s work force of 50,000
> has participated in at least one [meditation or yoga] class,
> and they report, on average, a 28 percent reduction in
> their stress levels, a 20 percent improvement in sleep qual-
> ity and a 19 percent reduction in pain. They also have
> become more effective on the job, gaining an average of
> 62 minutes per week of productivity each, which Aetna
> estimates is worth $3000 per employee per year. Demand
> for the programs continues to rise; every class is over-
> booked.[17]

■ Eileen Fisher

Eileen Fisher, head of the clothing company that bears her
name, has integrated mindfulness and meditation into the values of her organization as well as her own personal daily regi-
men. According to Fisher: "For the past several years I've been
thinking about the balance between work and home life, between the inner and outer life. I've learned that the only way I
can be fully present for someone else is if I first take care of
myself. I take time every day, even if it's just a few minutes, to
clear my mind—to stop, to stretch, to breathe. It helps me remember what's important."[18] The leadership culture at the
company is much more collaborative and consensus-based than
at most, using strategies like appreciative inquiry (a change

management approach that focuses on identifying what is working well, analyzing why it is working well, and then doing more of it) and relational practice (which places value on mutuality, interdependence, and sensitivity to emotional context)—models that tie perfectly to the mindfulness practice of compassion and awareness.

In addition to an employee stock ownership plan and profit-sharing bonus, the company provides a reimbursement of up to $1000 per year for wellness-related expenses including products, massage, acupuncture, gym memberships, exercise equipment, and wellness retreats. Among the programs offered at the office are free yoga, Pilates, and tai chi classes; mindfulness and financial well-being workshops; a quiet space for meditation; and 10-minute desk-side neck and shoulder massages. The company encourages personal growth through learning with an additional reimbursement of up to $1000 per year for classes, workshops, and training sessions. Employees have access to a variety of therapeutic practitioners, including massage, acupuncture, reflexology, astrology, hypnotherapy, and nutrition, for which employees can use their wellness and education reimbursement benefit.[19]

All of these investments in employees are part of a larger social and environmental business strategy, and they have put Eileen Fisher on the Great Places to Work Institute's leaderboard for several years running. Making this list is more than just good marketing. A study of companies that made this list over the last 30 years shows they enjoy significantly lower voluntary turnover and better financial performance than industry peers.[20]

▧ General Mills

The food company General Mills, with its world headquarters in Golden Valley, Minnesota, has been a pioneer in bringing mindfulness and meditation to the workplace, having given the green light to set up a program in 2006. The company's mindfulness program is voluntary, and it has thus far trained 500 employees and 90 senior leaders. The offerings vary. There is a four-day retreat for officers, directors, and senior managers; two-day training for new managers; and a two-hour class running seven consecutive weeks, which is open to all employees. There are also weekly meditation sessions. In every building on the General Mills campus, there is a meditation room, equipped with a few cushions for sitting practice, and yoga mats, where employees duck in to grab a few minutes of equanimity between their meetings. According to the company's research, 80 percent of participants said they felt the meditation and stress reduction program has improved their ability to make better decisions.

The program began as a side project by one executive, Janice Marturano, formerly General Mills' deputy general counsel, and it has really transformed the culture of the company. Marturano claims, "It's about training our minds to be more focused, to see with clarity, to have spaciousness for creativity and to feel connected. That compassion to ourselves, to everyone around us—our colleagues, customers—that's what the training of mindfulness is really about."[21]

■ BlackRock

Golbie Kamarei, a former global program manager for sales excellence for BlackRock (an investment management firm), started meditating on her own and was inspired to share her positive experience at her office in New York City. She worked with leadership and started a weekly program, informally inviting others in the office to join her in a conference room. What began with a few people in one office grew to 1,300 people (12 percent of BlackRock employees) in 30 cities and 17 countries.

What is incredible about Kamarei's story is that she started her meditation practice in a very grassroots way, with just a few people at a time, plus the fact that it took off like wildfire in a company within the financial services industry—typically conservative and slow to adopt new programs like hers. Clearly, she is tapping into a demand for releasing stress at the office. She knew it would be important to collect some quantitative data in a financial services firm to prove results. So she sent out a survey and found that of those who meditated as part of this corporate initiative, 91 percent believe it positively added to the culture; 66 percent experienced less stress or were better able to manage stress; 63 percent were better able to manage themselves at work; 60 percent experienced increased focus, increased mental resilience, and better decision making; 52 percent better managed relationships with peers at work; and 46 percent experienced increased innovation and creativity.[22]

STRATEGIES TO REDUCE STRESS AT WORK

When work is stressful, it is often because we feel aspects of our job are out of our control or overwhelming. Our mind is going a thousand miles a minute with everything we have to do. Quieting it down to process information more carefully and thoughtfully is not only important for reducing stress but for making good, sound business decisions. In addition to regular meditating, a mindful and less stressful work practice today is about managing in the present moment and managing workload in general. Here are some strategies for leaders and managers to help their teams focus and keep perspective at work. Each of these involves changing organizational culture, the work process, or the physical work setting in some way.

■ Develop a Stress Management Program

Depending on resources and the interest of leadership and employees, a successful stress management program might involve meditation, yoga or fitness classes, individual coaching (on stress, finances, time management, etc.), or even bringing pets to work. The best and longest lasting programs involve engaging employees, both in setting up the programs and in sustaining them over time. It also helps tremendously to have a leader involved who supports the program—not there just to approve the program or sign a check, but someone willing to take advantage of what the program has to offer and participate enthusiastically in its development. Leaders who champion these efforts—like Bill Duane, Chade-Meng Tan, Mark Bertolini, Eileen Fisher, Janice Marturano, Steve Jobs, and Golbie Kamarei—were not all from the C-suite, but they had some organizational pull. They also were willing to take some risks and be associated with their program's success or failure.

Some of the classes or programs currently being offered by leading organizations with the purpose of reducing stress and increasing productivity include meditation, mindfulness, yoga, tai chi, qigong, nutrition counseling, personal training, financial planning, time management, stress management, psychotherapy, massage, and sleep counseling.

◼ Encourage Employees to Focus on One Task at a Time

Multitasking is not really doing two things at the same time. It is actually *rapid task switching.* Brain scans during task switching show activity in four major areas. The prefrontal cortex is involved in shifting and focusing your attention and selecting which task to do when. The posterior parietal lobe activates rules for each task you switch to. The anterior cingulate gyrus monitors errors, and the premotor cortex is preparing for you to move in some way. Task switching takes longer and causes more errors than performing one task at a time. Peter Bregman, executive coach and author of *Four Seconds,* quotes several studies when he claims in the *Harvard Business Review* that multitasking leads to "up to a 40 percent drop in productivity, more stress, and a 10 percent IQ drop."[23]

Managers can help employees to reduce multitasking by planning team meetings or "check-ins" with employees at regular times at the beginning or end of the day so as not to disrupt their work; helping employees organize, plan, prioritize, and delegate their work; and creating behavior protocols to minimize unwanted disruption.

■ Get Rid of Email (or At Least Change How You Use It)

Sam Sidhu is the founder and CEO of Megalith Capital Management, a successful real estate and development company in New York City. He is a mover, a shaker, and then some. He runs a small team, all located in one office, and they work long hours. Sidhu started having back problems and difficulties staying asleep, and he came to terms with his addiction to devices. He realized he was spending 100 percent of the time he spent in the office just responding to emails—with no time for collaborating, thinking, or working on the next project. His team started exploring tools that would help them work more efficiently than email, and they adopted Slack and Asana. Using a combination of these tools has allowed his team to work on projects in a more streamlined fashion, without a lot of back-and-forth, saving stress and time. Sidhu claims to have recaptured at least five hours a week and saved "a day" of his team's time a week due to more efficient communication and streamlined meetings. He still uses email for external communication, but Megalith's interoffice email was dramatically reduced.[24]

■ Design Places for Psychological Restoration

Often, workplaces are designed to be denser and more open in order to increase collaboration and facilitate the "urban friction" that sparks creativity, innovation, and new business ideas. But this push, to cram employees into dense and highly open work environments without any "relief," has some serious drawbacks.

If you follow stories in the media about the problems with the open workplace, the most common issues are feeling crowded or trapped, disruption from unwanted noise, having visual distractions, and/or worrying about being taken by surprise. Being packed in like sardines is not good for mental health or creativity.

More sophisticated open workplaces are designed for small groups of up to 25 people, not a "sea of cubicles." Franklin Becker, a longtime researcher and faculty member at Cornell University's College of Human Ecology, finds that groups of 25 workers can more productively interact than larger groups.[25] In order to support groups of this size in the open, consider providing some enclosed spaces adjacent to the open areas that allow workers to perform quiet tasks, take confidential phone calls, have a private conversation, or conduct a team meeting. This supports choice and allows employees to retreat and restore energy levels, which, it turns out, is necessary for stress reduction, flow, and creativity.

When we are around people all the time, and because we are social animals by nature, we can often be distracted by others, which prevents us from reflecting on and processing what we have just experienced. Getting away from others regularly throughout the day is crucial for learning and for clearing our brains so we can focus. Sally Augustin, an environmental psychologist, refers to this as *psychological restoration*. Good places for restoration in workplaces should have some combination of views to the outdoors, plants, natural materials, daylight, nature sounds, and/or minimal technology disruption.

In addition to enclosed or private spaces, consider also providing meditation rooms, yoga studios, Zen gardens, libraries, areas to walk outside, or other spaces designed to encourage taking a mental break. Even if your company cannot afford to design and build special spaces for breaks, you might be able to remove furniture in an office or conference room and replace it with soft seating and hang pictures of landscapes. The most important factor in creating psychological restoration is creating a culture that supports it! If employees get evil stares for leaving their desk to go read for a few minutes or take a short walk, they are much less likely to take those needed breaks. Changing the culture requires senior leaders taking breaks themselves, and then encouraging their employees to do so.

■ Provide Choice for *Where* Employees Can Work

As mentioned in Chapter 3, choice is a particularly important factor in helping employees feel in control of their work, which impacts performance and health outcomes. Providing a choice as to where employees can work is a means to do that. Technology has greatly increased the ability of workers to get things done outside traditional workspaces. For example, many people can work effectively and efficiently at home, in a satellite office, on a plane or train, or in a hotel room, park, or coffee shop. The key is determining what activities are best suited for more flexible work and providing employees with the right tools to be mobile, like a laptop, cell phone or softphone, VPN connection, and with the necessary security controls in place. More portable tasks might include making personal or business calls, reading and responding to email, reading industry magazines or work materials, or just doing some deep thinking, which might be hard to do at the office.

Many employees who are given permission to work at home or away from the office find that they can get more done, usually because they are naturally able to work through tasks without interruption. Studies show that when employees are given the flexibility to move around the workplace to find "quiet space," or allowed to work from home, they are not only more productive and less stressed but they work more hours and are more satisfied with their job. According to a Gallup Panel Workforce survey of 13,968 full-time U.S. workers done in 2012,

"Remote workers log an average of four more hours per week than their on-site counterparts. Despite working longer hours, working remotely seems to have a slightly positive effect on workers' employee engagement levels."[26]

■ Provide Choice as to *When* Employees Can Work

Flexible work schedules are an alternative to the traditional 9 to 5, 40-hour workweek. They allow employees to vary their arrival and/or departure times. Under some policies, employees must work a prescribed number of hours per pay period and be present during a daily "core time." Other arrangements include job sharing, where a full-time position is split between two coworkers by mutual agreement and benefits are given in proportion to the number of hours each person works. Another option is a compressed workweek where employees complete their weekly work hour requirements in fewer than five days. Whatever the arrangement, employee choice is at the center of these policies.

■ Allow Employees to Choose *How* They Work

It may be too difficult for your company to allow certain employees to choose where and when they work, but helping them change the way they carry out their workday might be a strategy to help them cope with stress and the daily grind. Even if the company does not provide adjustable desks, it may be possible for employees to change position or location in their workplace so that they can work while standing, like working at a table in the break room or attending a "stand up" or walking meeting. Making small adjustments—like moving or adding a monitor, turning on a task light, orienting furniture, or organizing the work being done—can make a major difference in how employees feel about the health of their workplace.

The key when investigating any of these workplace strategies is to study which ones might work best for your organization's culture and the needs of the workforce before they are rolled out. I highly recommend doing some analysis of your workforce before diving in, like conducting interviews, focus groups, and observations, as well as visiting companies that have already implemented such strategies. Nothing beats visiting a space and talking to leaders, managers, administrative staff, and workers who have already adopted a flexible strategy and worked out all the kinks. Also note that most of these strategies require change management and training to work well. A recent International Facility Management Association study identified several training requirements for new ways of working, such as the use of new devices, software, hardware, etiquette protocols, business processes, and meeting protocols.[27] Leaders and employees cannot change their behavior overnight, and people need help learning how to work differently as individuals and as teams. Otherwise, employee flow is greatly disrupted.

■ Encourage Employees to Take Their Vacation

U.S. employees use only 51 percent of their eligible paid vacation time and paid time off, according to a recent survey of 2,300 workers who receive paid vacation. The survey was carried out by research firm Harris Interactive for the career website Glassdoor. Even more frightening, 61 percent of Americans work while they are on vacation, despite complaints from family members; one in four report being contacted by a colleague about a work-related matter while taking time off, while one in five have been contacted by their boss during vacation.[28] America has been referred to as the "no vacation nation" lately, and this constant working is negatively impacting individuals and their employers. According to John de Graaf, who made a documentary about overworked Americans called *Running Out of Time*, there is a high cost to not taking vacation. "Women who don't take regular vacations are anywhere from two to eight times more likely to suffer from depression, and have a

50 percent higher chance of heart disease," he says. "For men, the risk of death from a heart attack goes up a third."[29]

Managers can greatly improve the quality of their employees' lives, reduce their stress, and improve their performance by encouraging staff to take time off on a regular basis. Also, they can ensure that their employees relax away from work if there are protocols in place that allow employees to take time off and fully unplug without consequences, such as a rule that "no email should be sent to employees on vacation."

■ Encourage Laughter in the Workplace

It may sound a little strange to suggest this, but evidence shows that laughter can be a powerful tool for stress reduction and engaging employees. Kaiser Permanente encourages employees to attend "Laughaceuticals," which are interactive workshops where participants engage in improvisational theater techniques and exercises to have fun, laugh, and play. Throughout the workshops, ideas and statistics supported by research are discussed to raise awareness about the importance of laughter for well-being.[30] Kaiser Permanente sees these workshops as much more than stress reduction for its employees. The physical and mental health benefits of laugher are profound. It boosts stress hormones, decreases pain, relaxes muscles, prevents heart disease, boosts immunity, eases anxiety and fear, relieves stress, improves mood, and enhances resilience. Kaiser also sees the social benefits of laughter programs, including their ability to strengthen relationships, enhance teamwork, diffuse conflict, and promote group bonding—all helpful strategies for boosting business performance.

■ Allow Employees to Bring Their Children to Work

Companies that provide child care facilities for employees score huge bonus points with parents because it can save them time and stress trying to find child care independently. Having these facilities nearby can also allow workers to stay at work a little longer, which helps increase their productivity. That said, these facilities require people to manage and operate them, and they occupy a certain amount of space, which is not always practical. A number of companies are exploring more informally letting employees bring children to work, maybe not all the time, but when other child care falls through, like on snow days or between summer camp sessions. Some companies provide separate rooms or areas for children to hang out or do homework, with pencils, crayons, paper, a TV, video games, books, soft seating, tables, and windows, if the children need to be at work for extended periods. Spaces like this need to be monitored and, when younger children are present, it is essential to have a babysitter there. If you don't have a space for children or a strategy for accommodating them at work, consider enhancing your company's work-at-home policy in order to deal with the realities of having employees with young children (as well as aging parents or other personal responsibilities).

■ Allow Employees to Bring Their Pets to Work

A growing body of evidence suggests that pets in the office can have health benefits, improve morale, and even increase collaboration among workers. In some cases, pet owners may work longer hours if they don't feel as if they have to rush home to let their dogs out at the end of the day. Randolph Barker, professor of management at the Virginia Commonwealth University School of Business, has studied dogs in the workplace and found that bringing them to work resulted in a measurable decline in stress among workers over the course of a day.[31] Companies that allow bringing dogs to work include Amazon, Ben & Jerry's, Google, Clif Bar & Company, and Procter and Gamble's Pet Care Division.[32] Many companies that allow dogs have a strict policy restricting cats at work (cats and dogs don't always get along).

In summary, there are so many areas of research in this book that have helped me improve my own health, work performance, and overall happiness. But this particular area of research—of understanding the human mind and how to quiet it down and make room for clear thinking and focus—has been the most difficult, most unexpected, and most transformative path. I have been amazed and delighted to meet people from all walks of life who have seen their lives greatly improved by leveraging stress reduction techniques to improve their happiness, engagement, and productivity—all without a knife or a pill. That said, sometimes stronger interventions are necessary and appropriate to reduce stress and improve mental health, and smart employers are sensitive and supportive of that too.

6

Sleep Your Way to Success

WHEN I WAS PREGNANT WITH my first child, I remember getting plenty of advice from parents everywhere, to the point that it was highly annoying. It's not that I did not appreciate people caring, but when I was pregnant and hot and uncomfortable, thinking too far ahead was a strain. Most of the advice I got is still a big blur with the exception of one nugget of information I received from a colleague that has stuck with me to this day. He said, "Enjoy sleeping, Leigh, it's the last time you'll get it." "Ever?" I asked. "Yes. By the time you get through the baby phase and actually sleep through the night, you'll be staying up worried about your children forever more." At the time, his kids were out of college, so this made the advice particularly compelling—and disconcerting. With two young children now in tow, I can truly recognize the importance of sleep and how it affects my work.

The issue of poor sleep is a growing one. Sleep problems—including insomnia, obstructive sleep apnea, restless leg syndrome, and sleep deprivation in general—affect up to 45 percent of the world's population, according to the World Association of Sleep Medicine. A National Sleep Foundation survey suggested that most people around the world—from the western Pacific to North America to Europe—are not getting enough sleep. Less than 50 percent of people in Mexico, the United States, Canada, the UK, and Germany report getting a good night's sleep every night and "almost every night" on weeknights. And only 54 percent of Japanese participants said they consistently get a good night's sleep.[1]

The Centers for Disease Control has found that 50 to 70 million American adults are sleep deprived, and this impacts more than just work. The National Highway Safety Administration estimates that more than 100,000 auto crashes annually are related to fatigue. Insufficient sleep is also associated with several chronic diseases and conditions, such as diabetes, cardiovascular disease, obesity, and depression.[2] According to the National Institutes of Health, sleeplessness creates $16 billion in annual health care expenses and $50 billion in annual lost productivity, and that's just in the United States.

Professor Charles A. Czeisler from Harvard Medical School, an expert on the subject of sleep, was asked about the impacts of sleep deficit on corporations. He states:

> Executives I've observed tend to burn the candle at both ends, with 7 a.m. breakfast meetings and dinners that run late, for days and days. Most people can't get to sleep without some wind-down time, even if they are very tired, so these executives may not doze off until 2 in the morning. If they average four hours of sleep a night for four or five days, they develop the same level of cognitive impairment as if they'd been awake for 24 hours—equivalent to legal drunkenness.[3]

Sleeping is not just a concern for jet-setting executives. It is a concern for all employees, particularly those not working during the daytime. Shift workers—about one in five Americans—work nontraditional hours (not the typical hours of 9 a.m. to 5 p.m.). In China, shift workers are 36.1 percent of all manufacturing workers and 19.3 percent of service workers. They are roughly 14 percent of workers in the UK and 17.7 percent of workers in EU countries.[4] Difficulty falling asleep is a common effect, as is obtaining quality sleep during the day hours. Shift workers, in general, report more sleep-related accidents and illnesses.[5]

Employees working on little sleep are just plain bad for business. In a study from the *Journal of Occupational and Environmental Medicine*, more than 4,000 employees at four U.S. corporations were surveyed about sleep patterns and were classified into four categories: insomnia, insufficient sleep syndrome, at-risk, and good sleep. Compared with the at-risk and good sleep groups, the insomnia and insufficient sleep syndrome groups had significantly worse productivity, performance, and safety outcomes. The insomnia group had the highest rate of sleep medication use; the other groups were more likely to use non-medication treatments. Fatigue-related productivity losses were estimated to cost roughly $2000 per employee annually.[6]

SLEEP ARCHITECTURE

The study of sleep and sleep deprivation is still in its early stages, but there is growing research on the topic that sheds light on its importance to our general health and performance. Studies show that we need 7 to 8 hours of sleep a night, yet Americans get an average of 6.7 hours on weekdays. Not getting the right amount can be a problem. For example, getting too much or too little sleep contributes to weight gain. Specifically, short-duration sleepers are 35 percent more likely to experience weight gain, and longer-duration sleepers are 25 percent more likely to have a substantial weight gain. And our brains are very active when we sleep. We learn and make connections more effectively when we are asleep than we do when we are awake. Each night of sleep allows our brains to process what we learned the day before. As a result, we are more likely to remember what we learned if we sleep well.[7]

Getting a good night's sleep is a foundational element of health. It is something we can't outsource or purchase. It affects virtually every aspect of cognitive performance, physical performance, and creativity. To create good work policies and rituals for employees, it is helpful to first know how sleep works, sometimes referred to as *sleep architecture,* or the structure and pattern of sleep over a 24-hour period. There are many elements to it, which are fairly medically complex, but for our purposes, it's important to understand some key components, particularly sleep cycle, homeostasis, and circadian rhythm.

Sleep Cycle

During sleep, the human body cycles between rapid eye movement (REM) and non-REM (NREM) sleep several times during the night. Typically, you begin the sleep cycle with a period of NREM sleep, followed by a very short period of REM sleep, which is when dreams occur. A completed cycle of sleep consists of a progression from Stages 1 to 4 of NREM sleep before Stage 5 (REM sleep) begins. Then the cycle starts over again, beginning with Stage 2:[8]

> *Stage 1.* During this NREM phase, your eyes are closed, but you can be awakened without difficulty. If aroused from this stage of sleep, you may feel as if you have not slept. Stage 1 may last for 5 to 10 minutes.

> *Stage 2.* The second stage of NREM sleep lasts for about 20 minutes. Your brain begins to produce very short periods of rapid, rhythmic brain wave activity known as sleep spindles. Your body temperature begins dropping and your heart rate slows down. At this point, you prepare to enter deep sleep.

> *Stages 3 and 4.* These are deep sleep stages, with Stage 4 being more intense than Stage 3. These stages are

known as slow-wave or delta sleep. If aroused from sleep during these stages, you may feel groggy or disoriented for a few minutes. During these deep stages of sleep, the body repairs and regenerates tissues, builds bone and muscle, and appears to strengthen the immune system.

▶ *Stage 5.* This first phase of REM sleep typically lasts 10 minutes. It is followed by other periods of REM sleep, with each phase lengthening; the final one may last up to an hour. Intense dreaming occurs during REM sleep as a result of heightened brain activity, but paralysis occurs simultaneously in the major voluntary muscle groups. The percentage of REM sleep to total night's sleep is highest during infancy and early childhood. During adolescence and young adulthood, the percentage of REM sleep declines. Infants can spend up to 50 percent of their sleep in the REM stage of sleep, whereas adults spend only about 20 percent in REM.

The entire sleep cycle, from Stages 1 to 5, typically lasts between 90 and 110 minutes. Over the course of the night, the amount of time we spend in a particular stage of sleep begins to shift. During the first two or three sleep cycles, we spend most of our time in deep NREM sleep (Stages 3 and 4), whereas during the final two or three sleep cycles, we spend more time in REM sleep accompanied by lighter NREM sleep. Regardless of when you fall asleep, people tend to experience more NREM sleep in the earlier hours of the night (11 p.m. to 3 a.m.) and more REM sleep in the early hours of the morning (3 a.m. to 7 a.m.).[9]

So to generalize, a highly restorative time for our *bodies* is earlier in the night, while our *mind* is most restored later, in the early morning, with additional time in REM sleep. It is during this REM time that our brains are piecing together everything we have learned during the previous day; interestingly, this is also when we can accomplish creative problem solving. Several studies have connected sleep to creative problem solving. In a study at the University of Lancaster, participants were presented with a set of associated tasks that varied in difficulty. After a period of sleep, wake, or no-delay, participants reattempted previously unsolved problems. The sleep group was able to solve more difficult problems than the other groups, but no difference was found for easy problems.[10] Another study, from the University of Luebeck, asked subjects to complete math problems that relied on algorithms, but hidden deep within the formulas was an elegant arithmetical shortcut. About 25 percent of the subjects discovered it on their own, but that figure jumped to 59 percent when volunteers were given a chance to get eight hours of sleep and then come back to solve the problems. [11]

■ Homeostasis and Circadian Rhythm

Sleep is regulated by two body systems: sleep/wake homeostasis and circadian rhythm. When we have been awake for a long period of time, sleep/wake homeostasis tells us that it is time to sleep. It also helps us maintain enough sleep throughout the night to make up for the hours of being awake. If this restorative process existed alone, it would mean that we would be most alert as our day was starting out, and that the longer we were awake, the more we would feel like sleeping. In this way, sleep/wake homeostasis creates a drive that balances sleep and wakefulness.

Our internal circadian rhythm or biological clock, on the other hand, regulates the timing of periods of sleepiness and wakefulness throughout the day. The circadian rhythm dips and rises at different times of the day, so our strongest sleep drive generally occurs at night between 2 a.m. and 4 a.m. and in the afternoon between 1 p.m. and 3 p.m., though there is some variation. The sleepiness we experience during these circadian dips is less intense if we have had sufficient sleep, and more intense when we are sleep deprived.

The circadian rhythm is controlled by a part of the brain called the suprachiasmatic nucleus (SCN), a group of cells in the hypothalamus that respond to light and dark signals. From the optic nerve of the eye, light travels to the SCN, signaling the internal clock that it is time to be awake. The SCN signals to other parts of the brain that control hormones, body temperature, and other functions that play a role in making us feel sleepy or awake. In the morning, with exposure to light, the SCN sends signals to raise body temperature and produce hormones like cortisol. The SCN also responds to light by delaying the release of other hormones like melatonin, which is associated with sleep onset and is produced when the eyes signal to the SCN that it is dark. Melatonin levels rise in the evening and stay elevated throughout the night, promoting sleep. Although circadian rhythms are built-in, they can be adjusted to the local environment by external cues, primarily daylight. The early morning sun contains blue light that is a trigger to decrease the release of melatonin so that we can start our day. At the end of the day, when it gets dark, this is a trigger to begin the release of melatonin, making us sleepy.

STRATEGIES TO IMPROVE SLEEP

I realize that this book is all about work and the workplace, and that sleep is something we normally do at home, so why focus on it here? Because poor sleep is not just bad for our health: It's really bad for business (or good for business, if your business involves helping customers sleep). The sleep assistance industry—including pills, medical devices, consultants, and special mattresses and pillows—is growing rapidly in the United States and is currently at $32.4 billion a year.[12] Many companies are engaging sleep specialists or medical professionals to come into their workplace as part of their company health plans. Interestingly, there are several strategies that employers can put in place during work hours to impact their employees' ability to sleep later on. Sleep experts recommend developing a sleep routine (sometimes called *sleep hygiene*) with specific rituals that you do every day and night to ensure you are getting and benefiting from a good night's sleep. Some sleep habits occur at home, some at the office, and some during travel for work. Regardless of where you are, sleep rituals should be practiced consistently.

■ Schedule Employees as Consistently as Possible

Sleep experts recommend that if you wake up at 7 a.m. every morning during workdays and get to bed by 10 p.m., you should keep roughly the same schedule during the weekend. Wide variances in your sleep schedule disrupt the body's ability to self-regulate. Large time variations between week and weekend schedules is referred to by German researcher Till Roenneberg as *social jet lag*, and he has connected it to increased weight gain. He claims, "The larger the discrepancy between social time and what your biological clock tells you to do, the more likely it is you are [overweight or obese]."[13] In addition to keeping wake-up and bedtimes consistent between work and weekend days, it is important to keep hours consistent across workdays. Shift workers are particularly at risk for sleep disorders and a number of chronic health issues because they are working against their body's biorhythms. However, there are strategies to help them sleep better, mentioned later in this chapter.

■ Encourage Employees to Go Outside, Especially Early in the Day

A good portion of our global workforce spends most of each day indoors, which essentially puts workers in a state of "light deficiency." We need more intense light to reset our clock. Light intensity is measured in lux units, and the outdoor environment can exceed 100,000 lux in particularly sunny climates. More typically, the illuminance level is around 10,000 on an overcast day in the winter and about 30,000 on a bright day in the summer. Indoors, the typical average is somewhere between 100 and 2,000 lux—considerably less.

Some sleep experts recommend being outside as much as two hours a day, but even going outside for 30 to 60 minutes during the day—say, over a lunch break or during a walking meeting outdoors—provides roughly 80 percent of what you need to "anchor" your circadian rhythm, according to Dan Pardi, a researcher with the Psychiatry and Behavioral Sciences Department at Stanford, and the Departments of Neurology and Endocrinology at Leiden University in the Netherlands.[14] The ideal time to go outside, in order to align our body clock, is during the morning hours up until mid-day when the sun is at its brightest, but any time during the day will help.

■ Encourage Employees to Exercise During the Day

Cardiovascular exercise (activity where you keep your heart rate up and your muscles pumping continuously for at least 20 minutes) deepens and lengthens sleep, but exercising vigorously within about three hours of bedtime can actually make it harder to fall asleep, so sleep experts encourage people to try to work out earlier in the day. Also, exercise has been shown to help with insomnia and is a great alternative to taking medication, especially because sleep drugs are so addictive. Part of encouraging employees to exercise during the day means having an organizational culture that doesn't make it uncomfortable for them to leave for an hour to go work out. As mentioned in Chapter 4, this may mean providing workout facilities, subsidizing memberships to a nearby gym, or finding creative ways to double up existing workspace for exercise or stretching.

■ Accommodate Your Workforce by a Window

If your employees do not sit by a window at work, encourage them to walk by windows (or get outside regularly during the day). Workers without windows in their office may have more difficulty sleeping. Researchers from the University of Illinois, Northwestern University, and the Hwa-Hsia Institute of Technology in Taiwan teamed up to investigate the role of workplace windows in aiding sleep. They recruited 49 office employees, just over half of whom spent the day in mostly windowless environments, while the rest enjoyed frequent exposure to daylight through windows. The results showed those with the most light exposure snoozed an average of 46 minutes more per night than their light-deprived colleagues. They also scored better on a sleep quality scale and reported fewer nighttime disturbances—and they were more likely to exercise, after getting a good night's sleep.[15] One gap in this study is that it does not account for the fact that many office buildings have exterior windows that reflect the light waves that naturally suppress sleep. Having views to a window, even from a distance, is good for stress reduction purposes, but to get the benefits of "melatonin suppression," we typically need to sit very close to one (like within 5 feet).

▪ Install Circadian Lighting

If your workplace does not have windows, or even if it does, consider installing a circadian lighting system that provides appropriate light waves to trigger wakefulness. (Some new healthy building certification systems, such as the WELL Building Standard®, incorporate this lighting system in their standard.) Circadian lighting in workplaces takes into account natural and artificial light, a certain intensity of light at the desktop height level, and the presence of high light levels for a certain amount of time during the day.

I recently visited Bishop O'Connell High School in Falls Church, Virginia, where the administrative staff are testing circadian lighting in several classrooms. The lighting systems and wellness study was designed by an incredibly smart team of people led by David Conrath, owner of Anthrospheres, LCC, an industrial designer and "human-centric innovator" who works with architects along with the Marine Corps shooting teams and other secure branches to keep them alert and mission ready.[16]

Conrath replaced the old fluorescent lightbulbs in the classrooms with "biologically corrected" LED bulbs that mimic natural daylight (LightingScience Awake/Alert™ series light fixtures) and also added Sun Tunnel™ skylights (from VELUX) that draw in natural daylight from the roof. The result was a very well-lit classroom, but not overwhelmingly so. I was amazed at how the natural and artificial light quality and color were so similar. We took a look at classrooms without the new bulbs, and it looked like they were lit with kerosene lamps by comparison! One of the engineering teachers I met has been teaching class at 7:45 a.m. in the same room at Bishop O'Connell for six years, but in the last year, with the new circadian lighting, he noticed a real difference: "My students are just more alert now. They have no idea we've installed these new lights, but I have noticed they are more focused and energetic." Conrath has just completed a study of the Bishop O'Connell students using these spaces, and he found that those who struggled in previous years seemed to be improving the most. The C- students improved two grade levels to B-! The school is anxious to continue the study for two more years to continue and monitor the results.[17]

Even if your workspace is lit at 500 lux, which is more than enough light for reading and most work tasks, it will not necessarily reset sleep schedule. The light that is important to our circadian rhythm is different from the light that is important to our visual system because of the spectral difference in the light sensitivity of our photoreceptors.[18] According to Conrath, "Most people think that circadian lighting has to do with the color of light, but circadian light waves are invisible to us. Special LED lights are required if we want to use them to increase our wakefulness or help us sleep."[19]

Many of the benefits of these lighting systems are still being quantified, but early results show increases in worker productivity, a higher sleep score, and a reduction in seasonal affective disorder (SAD). If there is one investment you make to improve the quality of your workplace, this one is probably it. Research led by Jennifer Veitch, PhD, principal research officer at the National Research Council of Canada, shows that people who perceive their office lighting to be high quality rate their space as more attractive, have a more pleasant mood, and show greater well-being at the end of the day. People experiencing "good" lighting also felt that their performance was better than when they were not experiencing "good" lighting conditions.[20]

▪ Set Devices to Change Light Levels over the Course of a Workday

Devices such as TVs, computer monitors, tablets, and smartphones with self-luminous electronic displays are major sources for suppressing melatonin production as they emit light similar to early morning daylight, thereby reducing sleep duration and disrupting sleep.[21] Install an application like f.lux on devices to mimic the lighting in your workspace at the office or at home. This app continually adjusts your computer screen to look like the room you're in, all day. In the morning, the screen is brighter like sunlight and when the sun sets, it is dimmer like indoor lighting.

▪ Provide Napping or Wellness Rooms

Napping is a wonderful option during the workday if you think that you are not getting seven to eight hours of sleep and are feeling sluggish, especially around mid-afternoon. Most sleep experts recommend that people take a nap for no more than 30 minutes (10 minutes to fall asleep, then 20 minutes of light sleep, or Stage 1 and 2 in the sleep cycle) so that they do not wake up feeling groggy and are more likely to sleep later that night.

A 2011 poll of 1,508 adults by the National Sleep Foundation found that 34 percent of respondents say their employers allow them to nap at work, and 16 percent say their employers also have designated napping areas. Wellness rooms are also becoming more prevalent in offices (rooms that are used for napping, lactation, or lying down if you do not feel well). Especially if you use a wellness room for lactating mothers, please make sure the space is on a reservation system (like Microsoft Outlook) has comfortable seating, a small refrigerator (for storing milk), and a solid lockable door, preferably one that says "occupied/not occupied" on it. It is not ideal to have people knock on the door when you are expressing milk, dealing with a migraine, or napping. "Sleep pods" might also be an option for napping, if rooms are not available. Companies like Google and Cisco Systems have tried these, and they are slowly appearing in airports as well. An example of one of these, the EnergyPod, reclines occupants to the optimal napping position while playing ambient sounds to help nappers drift into light sleep. (See Figure 6-1.)

If your office is in New York City, São Paulo, or San Juan, you can take advantage of third-party napping facilities like YeloSpa, where people can book rooms for a power nap, skin therapy, or massage. This business model is unique in that you pay by the minute for nap time, a facial, or a massage. You can add on perks like dry body brushing, a micro-current lifting treatment, or even reflexology. If you opt for a nap, the chairs are zero-gravity (so you don't feel heavy the way you do when you are tired) and your legs are raised above your heart to slow your heart rate. Then you are tucked in with a cashmere blanket and surrounded by dim, soothing light and sound. When it's time to wake up, the room simulates a sunrise so your body wakes up naturally, so no alarm clocks are needed.

Figure 6-1. MetroNaps® EnergyPod®. Photo credit: Nathan Sayers.

▪ Cut Out Caffeine Service by Late Afternoon

Caffeine enters the bloodstream through the stomach and small intestine and can have a stimulating effect as soon as 15 minutes after it is consumed. Once in the body, caffeine persists for several hours: It takes about six hours for half of the caffeine to be eliminated. Put up a note reminding employees that drinking caffeine past 4 p.m. can impact their sleep, make noncaffeinated beverages more attractive in break areas, or if it makes sense for your workplace, stop coffee and tea service in the late afternoon.

▪ Set the Example and/or Set a Policy for Employees to Unplug

Working late at night might seem like a good idea at the time, but when it comes to sleep, it can be really disruptive. According to Dan Pardi:

> There's a new type of shift work, where people go to work in the morning, they come home, they spend a little bit of time with their families, and then on some nights they go back to work on their computers until late at night. This is a pattern that many people in the modern workplace maintain. This new type of shift work significantly alters our internal rhythms because on some nights you're getting light exposure for hours later than the day before. This variability in light instructs your rhythm-setting centers to constantly change body rhythms to try to catch up to the new pattern."[22]

In December 2011, Volkswagen announced that its servers would stop sending emails 30 minutes after the end of employees' shifts, and they would start again half an hour before the person returned to work. If this strategy seems too draconian for your company culture to swallow, consider asking senior staff and managers to refrain from sending emails to their employees past 8 p.m. so they set the example for others in the organization. Alternatively, adopt new tools like Slack, Asana, Newforma, or other project management tools that allow teams to communicate differently, so employees don't feel the need to "push" information to their coworkers in off-hours.

■ Give Employees Time to Sleep on Tough Work Problems

If you have a really difficult problem you need to solve, encourage your teams to write it down at night and then sleep on it to take advantage of REM brain-power creativity. Reid Hoffman— an Internet entrepreneur, venture capitalist, and author, best known as the cofounder of LinkedIn—makes it a habit to write down difficult problems the night before he needs to work on them, particularly those problems that require some creativity like a product design, a strategy, or a business issue. Then, as soon as he wakes up, he spends the first 30 to 60 minutes of his day, sometimes even before he gets into the shower, working on that problem. He finds early morning to be a good time for him to focus (without email or phone call distractions) and to unleash his creative thinking.[23]

SHIFT WORK

Most of us would claim that work regularly robs us of sleep. Issues or relationships at work may stress us out, which can keep us up worrying at night. Or maybe we are working late, which prevents us from winding down at the end of the day so we have trouble turning off our minds before bed. But the most chronic and dangerous sleep issues emerge for shift workers, or those who follow a work schedule that is outside the typical 9 to 5 business day. In the past few decades, the United States and the world has become increasingly dependent upon shift workers to meet the demands of globalization and our 24-hour society. From a competitive standpoint, shift work is an excellent way to increase production and customer service without major increases in infrastructure.

Some of the most serious problems shift workers face are frequent sleep disturbance and associated excessive sleepiness. Sleepiness and fatigue in the workplace can lead to poor concentration, absenteeism, accidents, errors, injuries, and fatalities. The issue becomes more alarming when you consider that shift workers are often employed in the most dangerous jobs, such as firefighting, emergency medical services, law enforcement, and security. Some of the most notorious modern catastrophes, such as the nuclear reactor meltdowns at Three Mile Island and Chernobyl and the crash of the Exxon Valdez oil tanker, have been attributed to human fatigue. Shift workers are also more likely to drive while fatigued and almost twice as likely to fall asleep at the wheel.

According to the *International Classification of Sleep Disorders*, shift workers are at an increased risk for a variety of chronic illnesses such as heart disease and gastrointestinal diseases. It is not known whether this is related to the fact that shift workers are awake and active during the night hours or because they tend to get fewer hours of sleep (and less regular exercise) overall than traditional workers. Shift work sleep disorders are often circadian rhythm disorders because of the frequency with which shift workers suffer from sleep disturbance and excessive sleepiness in trying to adapt to a shift work schedule.[24]

If you manage a workforce that does shift work, consider the following to help your employees sleep better and be more productive on the job:

► Follow the sleep recommendations listed in this chapter, but adjust times for a typical shift work day.

▶ Do not schedule workers for a number of night shifts in a row.

▶ Avoid scheduling frequently rotating shifts, and when the schedule does need to change, allow workers several days to change their sleep cycle.

▶ Create a work environment where employees work together to help them keep alert.

▶ Keep the workplace well lit with bright lights to promote alertness.[25]

▶ Encourage employees to be active during breaks (take a walk, exercise, etc.).

▶ Do not assign tedious or boring tasks at the end of shifts when employees are apt to feel the drowsiest.

▶ Provide night-shift workers with amber glasses so that when they leave work in the early morning light, the glasses counteract the light waves that typically shut down melatonin production (don't encourage them to wear these if they are driving home, however).

SLEEPING ON THE ROAD

When traveling for work, getting a good night's sleep can be a challenge. You are lying in a different bed, in a different room from what you are used to, and possibly in another time zone. I cannot tell you how many times I woke up in the middle of the night while traveling for work and forgot what town I was in or where the bathroom was located. It typically takes me several minutes groping in the dark to figure it out, and then a long time to get back to sleep after waking up. Every new little light, every noise, even different sheets can really impede my sleep.

A number of hotels catering to business travelers are recognizing the importance of health and the sleep quality of their guests, which makes sense given they are in the business of sleep! Your organization's travel agency might want to investigate hotel options like these for your employees (or consider some of their sleep strategies in nap rooms at your workplace):

- ► EVEN Hotels, a new family of wellness-oriented hotels, feature athletic studios for cardio, strength training, and mat exercises. Guests can take spinning and yoga classes or join a morning run led by each property's chief wellness officer. In addition, rooms are designed for working, sleeping, and exercising. The desk can be moved around and the bed has an angled headboard to support your back while working. There are blackout shades on the windows and natural eucalyptus linens on the bed that keep you from getting too hot during the night.
- ► Turn-down service at the Four Seasons includes a room attendant dimming the lights, adjusting the temperature, putting on soothing music, and drawing the curtains. The hotel keeps a record of its guests' pillow preferences.
- ► At The Benjamin Hotel in New York, guests can peruse a pillow menu that includes pillows filled with buckwheat or satin, with names like "Swedish Memory" and "Lullaby." And guests can arrange for a "work-down call," in which the concierge rings them up an hour before bedtime reminding them to stop working and put away their electronic devices.
- ► The Sound Sleep Initiatives, put together by Park Hyatt Beaver Creek Resort and Spa in Colorado with Nancy Rothstein ("The Sleep Ambassador"), include several strategies to provide guests with an environment and services that support a great night's sleep (some for an extra charge). These include a special Sound Sleep TV Channel featuring specially composed music by sleep expert Dr. Jeffrey Thompson, which enhances a guest's ability to have restorative sleep; a Slumber Massage at

the resort's spa, which soothes body and mind, ending in a brief nap; slumber kits, which include an eye mask, essential oil for sleep, earplugs, and a sleep music CD; sleep-friendly food and beverage items on the hotel's restaurant and room-service menus; and oxygen canisters and humidifiers to help guests adjust to the Rocky Mountain altitude.

☯

It seems so simple when you say it—"Just get a good night's sleep every night"—but doing so requires breaking some unhealthy habits that are really ingrained into our work culture and lifestyle. For some organizations, and for many teams, this is a major cultural shift, but it is essential to worker health, happiness, and productivity.

In 2007, Arianna Huffington was at home on the phone and checking emails when she passed out, fell, and woke up in a pool of blood, with a broken cheekbone and a cut over her eye. She had been working 18-hour days building the Huffington Post website. After weeks of medical tests, doctors finally came back with a simple diagnosis: She was really, really tired. Now recovered, she tries to get more sleep and is grateful for the wake-up call that changed her life. The Huffington Post now has two napping rooms and is a proponent of taking naps and stopping work when workers get drowsy. As Huffington has said to many audiences, "My single most effective trick for getting things done is to stop doing what I'm doing and get some sleep."[26]

 Design the
Workplace
for Health

OVER THE YEARS, ENVIRONMENTAL PSYCHOLOGISTS have interviewed people of all ages and from across cultures, asking them which environments they consider to be the most pleasant. They discovered that we all have a marked preference for a very specific type of outdoor landscape. When researchers show their subjects pictures of a rain forest, deciduous forest, coniferous forest, African savanna, and desert, by and large, people choose the African savanna. The savanna images usually depict short grass, trees, shrubs, and water. There are a number of theories for why people prefer these images, but most experts agree that it is because we are comfortable in environments that tie us back to our ancestral roots in Africa.[1] Short grasses allow you to see animals (prey or predators) coming at you from long distances. Trees and shrubs provide shade and a resting place from the sun. Access to water is critical for drinking, bathing, and hunting animals that live in the water. (The other strong preference we have is to be at a height looking down. We pay enormous prices for such views.[2] They give us a sense of security and serenity.) In the modern workplace, the "savanna preference" is an important consideration to help people feel safe and comfortable. It is not that we need to see predators approaching (unless, of course, we have a lion for a boss), but that our fear of confinement or being crept up on can be disconcerting and keep us from being our productive best.

OUR STRONG BOND WITH NATURE

Beyond our apparent preference to go back to our African home, humans generally have a strong desire to connect with nature in many ways. This preference, often referred to as biophilia, was introduced and popularized by the scientist Edward O. Wilson, commonly known as the "father of biodiversity." Wilson suggests that there is an instinctive bond between human beings and other living systems. In *Biophilic Design: The Theory, Science, and Practice of Bringing Buildings to Life*, authors Stephen R. Kellert, Judith H. Heerwagen, and Martin L. Mador describe the importance of nature for human productivity: "Nature is rife with sensory richness and variety in patterns, textures, light, and colors. All organisms respond with genetically programmed reflexes to the diurnal and seasonal patterns of sunlight and climate."[3]

Interestingly, a recent study conducted by a team of researchers led by psychologists Omid Kardan and Marc Berman from the University of Chicago (building on a body of prior research showing the psychological benefits of nature scenery) found that, controlling for income, age, and education, trees on the street had a significant independent effect on health. Specifically, they found that having an average of 10 more trees on a city block improves health perception in ways comparable to an increase in annual personal income of $10,000, moving to a neighborhood with $10,000 higher median income, or being seven years younger.[4]

Biophilia-based design can be manifested in many ways. The most obvious way is to incorporate real plants, water, and views to nature into the physical environment. Another way is to create *natural analogues*, which are one degree of separation away from true nature, such as materials and patterns that evoke nature, including artwork, ornamentation, biomorphic forms (evoking a living organism), or the use of natural materials. A third way to use biophilia is by the configuration of space—by organizing interior environments or synthetic outdoor landscapes using elements that are similar to, for example, the African savanna. In a report called *The Economics of Biophilia*, Terrapin Bright Green, an environmental consulting firm, claims: "Over the last quarter century, case studies have documented the advantage of biophilic experience, including improved stress recovery rates, lower blood pressure, improved cognitive functions, enhanced mental stamina and focus, decreased violence and criminal activity, elevated moods and increased learning rates."[5]

In June 2009, the New York City Department of Parks & Recreation opened the High Line, built on an abandoned elevated railway. If you visit this wildly popular urban design success story, you can experience first-hand the power of being in and among nature, despite the park's location across three bustling Manhattan neighborhoods. This park illustrates how access to the beauty and variety of nature is universally desired and valued.

Workplaces that promote human alertness and engagement evoke qualities of nature through the use of light, air, materials, color, spatial definition, movement patterns, openings and enclosures, and connections to the outdoors. "Nature" specifically refers to daylight, views of outdoor natural spaces, views of the sky and weather, water features, gardens, interior plantings, outdoor plazas, or interior atria with daylight, vegetation, and natural materials and décor.[6]

As if to turn its back on our human instincts, the modern work environment is often devoid of all the things that keep us alert and engaged. Acres of neutral-colored workstations, all with the same height and texture, do not support productivity or health. Spaces with daylight, window views to the outdoors, materials selected with sensory experience in mind (touch, visual change, color, pleasant sounds, and odors), spatial variability, change in lighting levels and use of highlights, and moderate levels of visual complexity are exactly what we need to be our productive best.[7] When the work environment is not stimulating, we lose focus and creative drive. An environment devoid of sensory stimulation and variability can lead to boredom, passivity, and even the taking of sick leave.[8]

In two studies of office workers, Lisa Heschong, an architect and researcher specializing in the impacts of day lighting on human performance, found that those with full window views, especially views of nature, performed better on a number of work tasks. One of the studies, conducted in a call center, found that workers with window views performed 6 to 7 percent faster (were able to handle more calls) than those without window views. In Heschong's second study, a field experiment, she found a positive correlation between window views and computerized memory and attention tasks. Furthermore, the quality of the view mattered. Those with full, high-quality views of natural vegetation performed 10 to 25 percent better on these tasks than those with a limited or artificial view.[9]

Another example of the importance of daylight and views is a study of an office building at the University of Oregon. Thirty percent of the office space in the building overlooked trees and a manicured landscape; 31 percent of the office space overlooked a street, building, and parking lot; and 39 percent of the offices were on the interior of the building and had no outside view at all. Occupants with views of trees and landscape took an average of 57 hours of sick leave per year, compared with 68 hours per year of sick leave taken by employees with no view. (Those with a view of a street, building, and parking lot ranked somewhere in the middle.)[10] Several studies have also been done showing a decreased length of stay for hospital patients in rooms lit with sunny daylight when compared to those in dull rooms with artificial lighting. A seminal health care study by Roger Ulrich, Professor of Architecture at the Center for Healthcare Building Research at Chalmers University of Technology in Sweden, showed that on average, patients recovering from gallbladder surgery whose windows overlooked a scene of nature were released after 7.96 days compared with the 8.71 days it took for patients whose views were of the exterior walls of the hospital.[11] Increases in daylight exposure have also been shown to improve test scores in children.[12]

In Germany, the maximum depth of leased buildings (distance between exterior walls in at least one direction) is 8 meters (26 feet) to ensure that all occupants have exposure to daylight. Building codes in the United States are not quite this prescriptive, but green and emerging healthy building certifications give significant "points" to builders, owners, or tenants who provide the majority of building occupants with access to natural light and views to the outside.

BIG IRRITANTS AT THE OFFICE

I spend a great deal of time interviewing and surveying building occupants about what irritates them about their workplace and prevents them from being their productive best. By far, the issues that are brought up most frequently have to do with acoustics, crowding, indoor air quality, and thermal comfort. Sometimes this is due to the fact that they sit in an open office—a trend that is probably here to stay in some form or another—but often their issues stem from the fact that the building is old or designed poorly. In some instances, workspaces can be fixed only by new construction. That said, modifications of existing environments are often possible to create healthier, more livable, less stressful places to work.

■ Acoustics

Noise is an issue in almost every workplace environment. Workers need acoustic (and visual) privacy, when desired, for psychological restoration.[13] Interestingly, noise can enable or disable productivity, depending on individual preferences and the type of work being done. The key is our ability to control what we hear. Studies show that when people have a degree of control over the noise in their environment, they are less distracted by it.[14] Contrary to popular belief, noise interruptions during simple, mundane tasks can be just the stimulation needed to be more productive. Interruptions caused by noise during complex work, however, require a longer period of time to reorient, and continued interruptions are likely to have negative effects on mood that reduce the motivation to resume work.[15]

The U.S. General Services Administration published a comprehensive guide called *Sound Matters* analyzing acoustics in the workplace. In it, the authors state:

> Office acoustics is a key contributor to work performance and well-being in the workplace. The ability to find quiet times and places is essential to support complex knowledge work, while the ability to have planned or spontaneous interactions without disturbing others is necessary for team work and relationship development. Having speech privacy is necessary for confidential interactions and work processes. "Acoustical comfort" is achieved when the workplace provides appropriate acoustical support for interaction, confidentiality and concentrative work.[16]

Ideally, your workplace environment has been designed well for acoustics, with a mix of absorptive materials (through acoustical ceilings, fabrics, and carpets), blocking (through furniture systems, panels, walls, partitions, and screens), and covering (through sound masking). But even the most carefully designed workplace environments have acoustic issues from time to time. That is where behavioral modifications become important, such as discouraging the use of speaker phones in the open work environment, or encouraging meeting room use for groups of three or more people.

■ Crowding

When we feel crowded we feel stressed, which influences how satisfied we are with our workplace. The perception of space and whether a person feels crowded varies greatly by cultural background, individual preferences, and gender. For example, in the same conditions, men are more likely to feel crowded than women. Men have slightly better peripheral vision than women and are more likely to perceive others in the same space.[17] The height of the building also matters. People who work in high-rise buildings tend to feel more crowded than people who do not. This effect is reduced for people who are on the upper stories of tall buildings, likely because they have better views and access to daylight.[18]

■ Indoor Air Quality

Americans and people in other postindustrial countries spend an enormous amount of time—roughly 90 percent or more—indoors. As a result, the quality of the indoor environment has a significant influence on well-being, productivity, and quality of life.[19] Headaches and sickness are a common result of working indoors and having exposure to abnormal levels of carbon monoxide, carbon dioxide, volatile organic compounds, and other factors. Indoor settings often contain levels of pollutants that may be two to five times higher—and occasionally more than 100 times higher—than outdoor levels. Sources of indoor air pollution include combustion, building materials and furnishings, toxins used to clean surfaces, factors involved with maintenance, central heating and cooling systems, and humidification.[20] Indoor air is also impacted by the piles of paper and clutter that are lying around and collecting dust.

A study on the costs and financial benefits of green buildings found that improvements in thermal comfort, lighting, and indoor air quality could reduce the incidence of respiratory illness, allergies, asthma, and sick building syndrome, and increase worker comfort.[21] Together, these building improvements would produce an annual U.S. savings or a productivity gain between $43 and $235 billion.[22]

■ Thermal Comfort

Thermal comfort is created through the right combination of temperature, good airflow, and humidity. A combination of these elements is required for physical comfort in the workplace. When you hear people complaining about temperature in their office, chances are that airflow and humidity are also part of the reason. The ideal temperature in office environments is 70.88° Fahrenheit (21.6° Celsius), with a 1–2 percent decrease in performance for every 1.8° F (1° C) above or below.[23] Slightly lower temperatures are associated with higher accuracy on simulated tasks and reduced sick leave.[24] Personal control over ambient conditions, especially temperature, increases productivity. One research study tracked workers in an insurance company as they moved to a new building with advanced thermal controls in their workstations. The study found that productivity increases of 2.8 percent could be attributed to the new workstations.[25]

HUMAN FACTORS AND ERGONOMICS

Workplaces that are designed for and around the physical constraints of the human body are more likely to be comfortable and flexible and to support productivity over time. This is because they take into account the needs and limitations of the people who occupy them. *Human factors* is an area of workplace psychology that focuses on a range of topics including ergonomics, workplace safety, the reduction of human error, product design, human capability, and human-computer interaction.

According to the American Academy of Orthopaedic Surgeons, musculoskeletal disorders (MSDs, which include back pain, arthritis, bodily injuries, and osteoporosis) are reported by people in the United States more than any other health condition.[26] The U.S. Bureau of Labor Statistics reports that MSD cases accounted for 34 percent of all injury and illness cases in 2012, with employees spending an average of 12 days away from work.[27] Much of this is caused by our behaviors at work, for example, sitting or standing for long periods of time, poor posture, repetitive movements, or some sort of trauma. Interestingly, as job-related psychological stress increases among office workers, so do complaints about physical pain, such as in the neck and back.[28] As we get more stressed, aches and pains bother us even more.

I recently conducted a workplace survey involving 3,600 U.S. employees across a wide spectrum of industries. An overwhelming 82 percent of respondents reported experiencing some type of physical ailment at work. The most common complaints—neck, back, and shoulder pain—were typical for workers sitting for long periods during the day. About half of those responding complained of pain in the neck, back, or shoulders, while a third reported headaches and eyestrain. Workers who stand for long periods of time at their job complained of hip, leg, and foot pain. The survey comments indicate that most of the complaints were the results of poor ergonomics or from being overly sedentary.[29]

Since a sizable number of injuries come from staring at a computer or device, it is highly likely that workers would feel much better if they made some minor adjustments to their posture, chair, keyboard, or monitor. In addition to minimizing injury, there is growing evidence that good posture also contributes to boosting mood. A recent study asked 110 university students to rate their energy levels, then walk in either a slouched position or in a skipping pattern. The students reported a decrease in energy levels after the slouched walk and an increase after skipping.[30] I'm not recommending skipping around the office, but sitting up or standing more often is a good start!

The U.S. Occupational Safety and Health Administration is a fantastic resource for understanding and helping prevent injuries on the job. If people in your office suffer from an injury or are concerned about the configuration of their work environment, I recommend checking out the OSHA website (www.osha.gov).

NEW BUILDING STANDARDS

Many of the strategies for creating a healthy and productive physical work environment stem from a recent push to make buildings greener or more environmentally friendly. Leadership in Energy & Environmental Design (LEED) is a building certification program whose credential has become a fairly common standard, but there are other building standards globally (BREEAM, Green Globes, etc.) that give explicit guidance to developers, designers, engineers, builders, and owners on ways for a neighborhood, campus, building, or workplace to reduce environmental impact. Within green building standards, there are also standards around improving the health of occupants. In many ways, what is good for people is also good for the planet. For example, using public transportation reduces carbon released into the atmosphere by cars, as well as increasing the likelihood that people meet their 10,000-a-day step target going to and from work. Putting plants into the work environment helps clean the air, but also, visual access to plants helps people to reduce stress and increase productivity. Reducing smoking improves health outcomes and also improves air quality. You get the picture. Lately, though, there has been a burst of new building standards and guidelines purely focused on improving human health.

The Active Design Guidelines, developed by several New York City agencies, provides strategies for designing neighborhoods, streets, and outdoor spaces to encourage active transportation and recreation, including walking and bicycling.[31] These guidelines also recommend ways for developers, builders, and architects to incorporate physical activity into the life of buildings through the use of stairs and building organization (centrally locating physical activity spaces like showers, locker rooms, secure bicycle storage, and drinking fountains) and making buildings "pedestrian friendly" through the use of multiple entries, canopies, and stoops.

The WELL Building Standard® is a performance-focused system for measuring, certifying, and monitoring features of the built environment that impact human health and well-being, including air, water, nourishment, light, fitness, comfort, and mind. The standard marries best practices in design and construction with evidence-based medical and scientific research and is the culmination of seven years of research in partnership with leading scientists, doctors, architects, and wellness thought leaders. The WELL Building Standard® is administered by the International WELL Building Institute, which was founded by Paul Scialla, a former partner with Goldman Sachs, to fulfill a Clinton Global Initiative commitment to improve the way people live by developing spaces that enhance occupant health and quality of life and by making the WELL Building Standard® available globally. The standard applies to commercial, residential, and institutional projects.[32]

The U.S. General Services Administration (GSA), the Centers

for Disease Control, and the City of New York (Department of Design and Construction and Department of Health and Mental Hygiene) have developed a new certification program called Facility Innovations Toward Wellness Environment Leadership (FIT-WEL), which will allow the GSA, other property managers, and the public at large to report their buildings' health and wellness amenities, which will be evaluated based on 63 scientific criteria that define a health-promoting building environment.[33]

STRATEGIES FOR CREATING A HEALTHY WORK ENVIRONMENT

Many of the strategies for creating healthy physical environments have already been referenced in earlier chapters, but there are many other tactics that can be applied. They include ways to increase natural light and views to nature and ways to reduce the many irritants that impact our productivity. Up to this point, this book has referred to ways to reduce noncommunicable or chronic diseases, but included below are ways to reduce communicable diseases as well.

▪ Maximize Natural Light in the Workspace

There are several strategies for increasing natural light in the workplace, the most important of which is to put people, not "stuff," by exterior windows if possible. Sometimes, in these massively deep buildings we may work in, it is not possible to put everyone by a window. If this is the case, place shared spaces by windows (like break areas, eating spaces, the cafeteria, workout areas, or corridors) so that all employees get access to windows and views at least some point during their workday. Use glass wherever visual privacy is not required, and paint walls and ceilings a lighter color or choose furniture that is lighter in color to reflect as much daylight as possible throughout the workplace. (See Chapter 6 for more information on artificial lighting strategies.)

Choose Workplaces with Volume

If you have a choice of where to locate your workplace, choose spaces with volume, particularly height. Taller ceilings reduce the feeling of crowding, provide more natural light (if they have big windows), and inspire creativity. Across several experiments, researchers have found evidence that high ceilings put people in a mindset of freedom, creativity, and abstraction, whereas lower ceilings prompt more confined thinking. In one study, marketing scholars Joan Meyers-Levy and Rui Zhu wanted to see whether the height of a ceiling had any impact on the way a person thinks, so they recruited test participants for a number of different experiments and modified the study rooms so that some had 10-foot ceilings and others had (false) 8-foot ceilings. Meyers-Levy and Zhu also hung up Chinese lanterns so participants would look up and, consciously or not, process the ceiling height. The researchers found that working in a high-ceiling environment put participants in a freer, more abstract mindset than did a low-ceiling setting.[34]

Integrate Plants and Views to Nature into the Work Environment

For several years, empirical studies have been done in Western and Eastern countries indicating that natural environments have therapeutic effects. Most agree that the therapeutic effect of nature is due to unconscious processes in the oldest, emotion-driven parts of the brain that inform us when to relax. In hospitals, where the direct outcome of views to nature can be more directly measured, patients have found relief from physical symptoms of illness or trauma, stress reduction, and increased levels of comfort dealing with an emotionally or physically tiring experience, as well as an improvement in the overall sense of well-being.[35] In workplaces, studies show that workers with views of nature feel less stressed and show higher levels of job satisfaction than those without them.[36] Frederick Law Olmsted, the American landscape designer of such spaces as New York City's Central Park, the Biltmore Estate in Ashville, North Carolina, and the Stanford University campus, once stated, "Natural scenery employs the mind without fatigue and yet exercises it; tranquilizes it and yet enlivens it; and thus, through the influence of the mind over the body, gives the effect of refreshing rest and reinvigoration to the whole [health] system."[37]

Integrating gardens, landscapes, and water features into the workplace is always a good choice, and there are many different types and varieties to suit climate, building configuration, and your budget. Consider ways to "green" your building grounds, entry garden, courtyards, roof, terraces, and atriums. Also consider how these spaces can be used in more ways than just walking through, such as meditation, holding meetings, or giving presentations. Figure 7-1 shows a "green roof" planted on what was an unsightly flat roof in the center of the Birch Bayh Federal Building and U.S. Courthouse in Indianapolis, Indiana, and Figure 7-2 shows an outdoor teaching and learning space at Wheaton College in Norton, Massachusetts. If you are not willing or able to go that far, consider placing potted plants or images of nature throughout the workplace. Interestingly, high-quality fake plants have a similar effect psychologically as real plants and could be an alternative if your workplace has a policy against live plants. Another related strategy is to strategically place wood, even "fake wood," into the work environment.[38] Studies show that materials that show wood grain are psychologically restorative as views to plants. (Note that painted wood is not as effective as wood that shows the grain.)[39]

If you want to really kick up the views to nature a notch within your workplace, install a living wall. Living walls are

Figure 7-1. Green roof on the Birch Bayh Federal Building and U.S. Courthouse, Indianapolis, Indiana, designed by EYP. © ESTO/David Sundberg.

Figure 7-2. Outdoor teaching and learning space, Wheaton College, Norton, Massachusetts, designed by EYP. © Robert Benson Photography.

made up of pre-vegetated panels or fabric systems that are attached to structural walls or frames. Living walls are particularly suitable for cities outdoors, as they allow good use of available vertical surface areas, but more and more often, they are being built into indoor environments to improve indoor air quality, minimizing sick building syndrome.

▪ Keep the Workplace Tidy

A clean desk policy is often associated with workplaces where there are shared seating arrangements (more than one person using a desk) or when there are security issues to consider by having papers in open view. But we should all adopt a clean desk policy for our health. Paper and clutter on the desk attract dust and mites, which trigger allergy attacks. Plus, having a clean work environment with only the files you need on your desk gives the appearance of having more space. Big piles of paper eat into the workspace and make us feel crowded. Studies show that working at a clean and neat desk encourages socially acceptable behaviors, such as healthy eating and generosity. Of course, these same studies find that working at a sloppy desk promotes creative thinking and stimulates new ideas.[40] Deal with clutter by containing it and provide employees with boxes or storage for their files and piles.

▪ Upgrade Furniture and Finishes

If your organization is moving into a new space or planning to refurbish an existing space, this is a perfect time to invest in furniture, carpet, paint, and other workplace finishes with low counts of volatile organic compounds (VOCs) that can trigger illness. Select providers with the GREENGUARD label that have met stringent third-party tests or the Carpet and Rug Institute Green Label Plus Carpet Program. The California Collaborative for High Performance Schools (CHPS) program also sets a high quality standard for interior materials and finishes.

▪ Train Employees How to Set Up Their Work Point to Minimize Muscle Strain

Check with an ergonomist and/or the manufacturers of furniture in your workspace to learn how furniture can be adjusted to accommodate different body sizes and postures. Chairs, primary and secondary work surfaces, monitors, keyboards, computer mice, and other equipment and devices are almost never set up correctly to support good posture and ergonomics. And seriously consider purchasing adjustable work surfaces. I am a huge advocate of sit-to-stand desks and believe they are worth the money, especially if workers are sedentary and need to be tethered to one spot for long periods of time. Studies show that even when you meet physical activity guidelines (like 150 minutes a week of moderate intensity physical activity), sitting for prolonged periods can still compromise metabolic health.[41] Some people have the physical stamina to stand for most of their day, but many others can stand for only two or three hours a day and certainly not all at once. Adjustable-height work surfaces accommodate these differences.

Don't forget about our eyes! All of our staring at computers causes us to blink 75 percent less than we would walking around, and to focus our eyes on a screen 20 to 40 inches from our face all day. Our eyes are muscles that need stretching just like any other muscle in the body. It is important to use them to view different depths and varying lighting levels during the day to stay "in shape."

▪ Consider Wall Construction, Materials, and Height

Acoustical issues in an open-plan environment are very common, but they are not unique to these environments. People in enclosed offices complain all the time about hearing the person next to them, usually because the walls are not fully insulated and/or the walls do not "go to deck" (meet the floor above). Interestingly, cubicles with really tall panels are the least effective acoustically. Because people can't see that they are interrupting others, they tend to talk more loudly. Once you lower the wall panels between seats (or make them transparent or translucent), people naturally turn down their voices.[42] No matter how tall the walls are, packing in people like sardines is difficult to mitigate acoustically in an open environment without sound masking and installing highly absorptive materials in the ceiling and floor.

Create Policies for Removing Distracting Behaviors in the Workplace

To reduce noise distractions, separate energetic spaces from quiet areas in the workspace, define policies for space use (e.g., use speakerphones only in enclosed rooms), and ensure that people are sitting near those with similar work patterns or subjects of study. A commonly used strategy is to agree on a "do not disturb" policy so that colleagues have cues about when they can approach each other. Some companies provide employees with noise-cancelling headphones, but white, brown, or pink noise phone apps are also readily available and can work just as well with a phone and set of earbuds. Also, think about the interruptions caused by technology. Consider suggesting that employees turn off the sounds on phones or devices that beep, chirp, or buzz when they receive texts, email, or messages from social media.

Use Color Strategically

Our psychological reaction to color varies based on national culture, religious background, and life experiences. However, there are some generalizations about how color is likely to be perceived, either overtly or subliminally, in the workplace.[43]

- ▶ Brighter colors (reds, as well as blues and greens) are associated with higher focus and task accuracy.
- ▶ Blue is calming and cooling, promoting mental control and clear, creative thinking.
- ▶ Pink lessens feelings of irritation, aggression, loneliness, discouragement, and burden.
- ▶ Red enhances feelings of strength and energy and is associated with vitality and ambition.
- ▶ Yellow makes people feel clear-headed and alert, allowing for clear thinking for decision making.
- ▶ Orange helps ease emotions and boost self-esteem and creates enthusiasm for life.
- ▶ Various shades of green have been linked to improved creative performance.[44]

Instead of using color based on your organizational logo or personal preferences, consider choosing it strategically to promote desired behaviors and feelings based on psychological reactions. Also, vary color use through your workplace. Use it as a design technique to identify circulation or the changing character of space.

▪ Reduce the Risk of Communicable Disease

When employees come into the workplace sick, they are very likely to spread their illness to colleagues and thus reduce organizational productivity. As tempting as it is for workers to power through and minimize the number of sick days taken, the overall health risk is not worth it. Researchers from the University of Arizona, Tucson, placed a tracer virus on commonly touched objects such as a doorknob or tabletop in workplaces. At multiple time intervals, the researchers sampled a range of surfaces including light switches, countertops, sink tap handles, and push buttons. They found that between 40 and 60 percent of the surfaces were contaminated within two to four hours.[45]

Interestingly, the specific layout of your workplace may also increase the risk of employees getting sick. Researchers from the Royal Institute of Technology in Sweden found that office type (enclosed, open, flexible, etc.) has an impact on how likely we are to pass on communicable diseases. The study found that workers who are assigned to open offices are much more likely to call in sick (for short-term leave) than people who sit in enclosed offices or flexible work environments (where people have a choice of where they work based on task).[46] The researchers believe this is because enclosed offices are more likely to be occupied by fewer people and the fact that workers in flexible work environments are mobile and more easily able to work at home when they don't feel well. Regardless of how your office is organized, consider adopting good hygiene policies, hiring a good cleaning company, and rolling out a "work from home" policy to include workers who are sick so that they do not infect their colleagues.

■ Improve Thermal Comfort and Air Quality

To help with temperature issues, consider providing zoned temperature controls or, if possible, individual temperature or air speed controls at each workspace (workstations, offices, conference rooms, etc.). Also consider providing operable windows or operable window coverings to maximize sunlight, airflow, and temperature control. To help with airflow issues, think about installing measuring stations that capture outdoor airflow rates to ensure that adequate ventilation air is introduced at all times. Some workers might want to use fans to control airflow (and also help drown out unwanted noise).

To help with air quality, invest in equipment with ENERGY

STAR labels and ensure that heating, ventilation, and air conditioning (HVAC) and other office equipment are checked and maintained on a regular basis. Consider installing CO_2 sensors in your space to ensure adequate air quality year-round. In addition, make sure work surfaces, carpets, and mechanical ducts are cleaned regularly. Use green cleaning products and equipment such as vacuum cleaners with HEPA filters. Note that you can unintentionally introduce VOCs into an otherwise healthy environment through a traditional cleaning program. Train cleaning staff on how they should use cleaning equipment and products, such as handling vacuum cleaners with HEPA filters or nontoxic chemical cleaners.

■ Use Smell to Increase Productivity (with Caution)

Here is an interesting tidbit. Most of the time when we talk about smell in the workplace, it is a bad thing, but not all smells are disruptive. In Japan, the Takasago Corporation carried out research into how smells affect the accuracy of typists. It found that 54 percent made fewer errors when they could smell lemon, 33 percent made fewer errors with jasmine, and 20 percent made fewer errors with lavender.[47] In another study, a significant positive relationship was evident between the presence of a lemon scent and mood.[48]

❨❩

In the words of Winston Churchill, "We shape our dwellings, and afterwards our dwellings shape us." The influence of the physical environment we occupy is remarkably strong. It can inspire and engage us just as easily as it can negatively impact our health, our motivation, and our ability to be effective and efficient. Smart companies see their work environment as an opportunity to influence behavior in a way that benefits employees and the bottom line, but also as a way of expressing the unique values, culture, and sense of community of the organization. And employees can literally see that investment: The space they sit in embodies it.

Also, it is important to be mindful that the physical environment has the power to educate in a way that other forms of media cannot. Think of it this way: It costs $250,000 for a full-page color advertisement in the *Wall Street Journal*, a page that is probably looked at by most readers for a total of only five seconds. But the buildings we sit in every day have an incredible amount of "advertising space" on walls, windows, roofs, ceilings, and floors for a significantly lower cost per square inch. Consider the work environment not as a finished product but a billboard and a laboratory for testing healthy strategies and innovations. If employees can see ideas at work in the office, they will learn something new and are more likely to try them at home and share their successes with others.

Create a Healthy Organizational Culture

A MAJOR REASON EMPLOYEES ARE not engaging in healthy behaviors at work has to do with organizational culture. Culture is often difficult to define or measure, but it controls our behavior in a very real way. Organizational culture, defined by consultants Terrence Deal and Allan Kennedy in their classic book *Corporate Cultures: The Rites and Rituals of Corporate Life* as "the way things get done around here," includes the organization's vision values, norms, systems, symbols, language, assumptions, beliefs, and habits. It is also the pattern of collective behaviors and assumptions that are taught to people new to the organization as a way of perceiving and even thinking and feeling.[1] Amazon has gotten some heat in the press recently about its highly innovative but very hard-working culture, where "workers are encouraged to tear apart one another's ideas in meetings, toil long and late (emails arrive past midnight, followed by text messages asking why they were not answered), and held to standards that the company boasts are 'unreasonably high.'"[2]

Culture has a profound effect on how we work—for example, how we behave in meetings, how we dress, whether we check our email before we go to bed, and whether we exercise during the day or wait until "after hours" to do so. It even impacts how stressed out we let ourselves get. And when we behave in a way that is not "culturally acceptable," we find out pretty quickly from the people around us. Sometimes culture is created intentionally; sometimes it's not. For example, I feel certain that a leadership team has never "officially" decided to roll out a policy declaring that all employees must check their phones for messages 24 hours a day, yet this has become the norm for many organizations.

I was at a conference recently and sat in on a work session where a woman from a large organization complained that she really wanted to take more personal time away from work, but she felt enormous pressure from leadership and her colleagues to work long hours and minimize vacation days. "At my company, people work really hard and it is frowned upon to take off work for any reason," she said.

This is not an uncommon phenomenon. I did some work for an investment management firm in New York City a couple of years ago, and I remember interviewing several portfolio managers and traders and getting a similar feeling about their culture. I was collecting data from them to help redesign their new office, and all the meetings I had with them were short and laser-focused. Everyone I met kept looking at their watches. "Time is money" was clearly part of this culture. When I spoke to the employees about health in the workplace, they were interested in anything that would keep them working effectively while staying glued to their desks. One trader mentioned that she took two weeks off to have a baby and felt that culturally, that was a perfectly reasonable amount of time to be away from the office. "I didn't really feel the need to breast-feed because I knew I would be coming back to working 80 hours a week immediately after my child was born," she said.

Now admittedly, this investment firm was a place where working hard and putting in a ridiculous amount of hours was par for the course. But even with this albeit extreme work ethic, we did manage to come up with some workplace strategies to encourage exercise and health, including sit-to-stand desks, places for taking showers (for those who worked all night, biked to work, or took a red-eye from London and needed to head straight to a meeting), a napping room, and a "green room" with lots of plants for reducing stress. We also rethought the free foods stocked in the kitchen so that employees would have good, nutritious food and drinks to get through their grueling 16-hour days.

Truth be told, a large number of organizations do not exactly support what the Robert Wood Johnson Foundation considers a "culture of health."[3] It's not that companies don't care about their employees—it's just that they don't exactly put employee health and wellness front and center. So when I visited the e-commerce company Next Jump's headquarters in New York City and The Motley Fool's main office in Alexandria, Virginia, I started thinking differently about what a healthy organizational culture really means.

BETTER ME + BETTER YOU = BETTER US

I visited Next Jump in New York at the suggestion of a couple of their employees whom I had met on my journey to find examples of super healthy workplaces. Their description of how their company addresses health and wellness intrigued me enough to want to visit one of the offices. After my visit to the office on a "culture tour"—led by Sarah Kalamchi and Peter Chiarchiaro, Next Jump's co-heads of wellness—I realized that this company was on the precipice of something really transformative. The people at Next Jump are integrating best practices from physiology, psychology, and sports science into the way they work and the way they run their business, and they are seeing some amazing results. But first, their story.

Next Jump was founded by Charlie Kim from his college dorm room at Tufts University in 1994. He went through school on financial aid and needed a way to pay for his phone bills to maintain a long-distance relationship with his high school sweetheart. To make some cash, he started selling student phonebooks that he and his friends distributed to schools in the Boston area. These books included advertisements, coupons, and menus that gave students discounts on products and services.

Soon after Kim graduated, the phonebook business became a dot.com business that grew to 150 employees in five offices. Then, around 2002, the bubble burst in the tech market and the company shrank to just four employees. This was a time of soul-searching for Kim and his small team. It was also an incredibly tough time, and Kim had a bloody nose for 60 straight days from the stress of it all. As the company rebuilt itself, Kim and his colleagues took time to think about the traits of the people they wanted to work with and that would be successful in their business. They concluded that they wanted people with humility who were not afraid to fail. They also began to refine their culture in tandem with their business strategy. They started to connect what they had learned from outside experts with their own experience, and they created a mission statement that has stuck with them to this day: Better Me + Better You = Better Us. Sarah Kalamchi explained it like this: "When you're on an airplane, you are directed to put the mask on yourself before you help others. *Better Me* is about taking care of ourselves before we can help others. *Better You* is about helping others, both inside and outside the company. When you are growing yourself (Better Me), you can better help others (Better You). This leads to *Better Us*, which is all about true wealth, leading a fulfilled life, and ultimately a better world."

Today, Next Jump has 200 employees in five offices with more than $2 billion a year in sales. The company has a five-year compound annual growth rate of 30 percent in e-commerce sales that grew to a 120 percent average from 2012 to 2015. The only thing leaders have changed in those three years (compared to previous years) was their deliberate focus on building a "captain creating machine"—in other words, leadership development programs. In order to create captains, the company increased its focus on all dimensions of employee health, including physical, emotional, mental, and spiritual.

They claim their investment in their culture and their people has led to this incredible growth, nine straight quarters of record-breaking results, and some of the lowest turnover rates in the technology industry (single digits as compared to a tech average of 30 percent). What does "investment in their culture" really mean? All of their employees spend 50 percent of their time working on their company culture and 50 percent working on the revenue side of their business. To Next Jump, culture work might include anything from taking a spin class, to coaching others, to donating skills or services to businesses in the community. Every culture initiative is an opportunity to further train and develop captains. They pay particular interest in giving back, adopting schools and nonprofits, and sharing what they have learned about improving their business with others.

The walls in Next Jump's workplace are covered with images of their leaders, their employees (practically all of their employees), business philosophies, awards, and quotes from the business gurus who most inspire them. At first glance, the office appeared a little cluttered, even messy, but after hearing their story and what they had accomplished, I realized that everything I could see had a story and real meaning to leaders and employees. Their culture is all about sharing what they have learned and reminding everyone who walks by what they are doing and why they are doing it. Their purpose and vision are hard to miss: It covers every square inch of wall space.

It's fair to say that at Next Jump, they take the health of their employees very seriously—not because they are worried about insurance costs, but because they see the physical and mental health of their employees as the enabler of their incredible business success. They call this way of thinking "altruistic self-ishness." The company cares about its employees, of course, but also knows that paying close attention to what employees eat, how often they exercise, their stress levels, and other health factors have an effect on financial results. Next Jump's leaders believe the health of their employees impacts the health of their business. It doesn't hurt their case that they have many testimonials from employees who were not so healthy when they came to Next Jump, then started to pay attention to their health and found their work performance improve. It only re-inforces the culture and encourages healthy behavior even more.

Next Jump uses a variety of strategies to support employees' performance. They lump all of these activities into time spent strengthening their company culture, which in turn impacts their revenue. Many of their culture-enhancing strategies are intended to improve the physical, emotional, mental, and spir-itual health of their employees, many of which were influenced by Jim Loehr from the Johnson & Johnson Human Performance Institute. It is clear that employee health is not just tacked on to business as usual, but integrated into their business prac-tices; it changes how they work. Here are just a few of the many strategies Next Jump has taken on that its leaders believe are critical to the company's success.

■ Leadership

Charlie Kim doesn't roll out new ideas in the business unless he and his leadership team have taken them on first. He gives back to his team and gives his time to many nonprofits, in many ways embodying the "servant leader" qualities he is trying to encour-age in his staff. Above the reception desk in the New York office is a sign that says in bold letters "Building a company that would make your mother and father proud." This is not exactly the first thing you would expect to see in the office of a multibillion-dollar company, but it is heartwarming.

■ Talking Partners

All employees choose a talking partner (what other organizations might call an accountability partner), or someone who might not be part of their team, and with a personality a little different from their own. Employees touch base with their talking partner daily, ideally in the morning, and chat about what is on their mind and blow off steam as they need to. The job of the talking partner is that of a co-mentor, helping to keep employees honest with themselves, helping them see things from a different perspective, and ensuring that they are meeting their physical, emotional, mental, spiritual, and project goals.

■ Easy, Healthy Choices

Next Jump kitchens are stocked full of high-nutrition, carefully portioned foods in containers they have specially made by their vendor. Healthy snack bins and bars are located throughout the workplace with red/yellow/green item labeling, indicating which items are more healthful than others. Breakfast and dinner on-site are free (some employees like to work a later shift because of personal choice or their commute). Lunch is subsidized, and it's free if you take a fitness class that day. If you want to eat or purchase unhealthy food, you are welcome to, but it requires leaving the building and searching for it. Food isn't the only thing offered to employees. There is a 31-bike spin studio, a sizable gym, and a physical trainer available to all employees.

■ Fitness Challenge

Next Jump asks all employees to work out for 20 minutes, two times a week. Even ping-pong games count as a workout. To incentivize employees to work out more, the company has a Fitness Challenge. Employees are split into several groups, and the teams that work out the most win prizes every week. The company publicizes "who is working out the most" online, in the gym, and even in the bathrooms! Next Jump also provides financial incentives in the form of 100,000 WOWPoints ($1000) to split among team members. WOWPoints can be used to shop at hundreds of online retailers. The Fitness Challenge combines teamwork, competition, and incentives and is an effective motivator. On average, more than 90 percent of employees meet the weekly fitness target the company has set.

■ Personal Coaching

At one point on my tour, we stopped by the gym, which seemed pretty sizable for such a small office. It was full of all of the equipment you might expect in a local neighborhood sports club. Then my guides took me to a more "experimental" area where they are engaging employees in various health and wellness techniques—all to help refine their coaching strategies, improve employee health, and, as a result, increase financial outcomes. In one of their tests, they asked me to lie down on a massage table, at which point they took my blood pressure. Then I stood up and they took my blood pressure again. This test, developed by Dr. Peter Gorman (inventor of the heart-rate monitor that goes into treadmills and stair master machines) is an indicator of stress levels. If your blood pressure is higher when you are standing up than when you are lying down, you are in a "state of growth" and could probably handle a few more responsibilities at work. If your blood pressure standing up is lower than when you are lying down, you are in a "state of survival," and you might want to take something off your plate—an indicator you might be operating beyond your capacity. I was in a state of survival mode when I took this test, and of course I immediately began to think of ways to outsource a few more tasks in my life.

Another tool they shared with me, again from Dr. Gorman, was called the OptoGait. This device basically looks like two five-foot plastic bars on the floor, each spaced parallel to each other and five or six feet apart. They have special sensors to calculate when objects touch the floor anywhere between them. The test is simple. First you march in place between each of the bars for 30 seconds. Then you march to a metronome at half the speed of your natural pace, then yet again at twice the speed of your natural pace. After some whirring, the PC attached to the OptoGait prints out results. Essentially, the OptoGait measures "flight and contact time," or the balance and consistency of steps. The results determine both the amount of effort expended and performance. Some people perform better in the exercise at a slower pace, some at a faster pace, which is a proxy for how they are likely to approach work tasks. According to my results, I performed better stepping slower than at my natural pace. According to Peter Chiarchiaro, it's likely that I perform better at work if I am given longer timelines and more flexibility to complete a task, rather than rapid deadlines. (This is totally true and now I have the results to prove it!) Next Jump uses this test and others as coaching tools to help their employees work at their best pace and with the right workload to maximize their performance.[4]

ACT LIKE A FOOL

When I walked into the reception area of The Motley Fool's headquarters in Alexandria, Virginia, I was greeted by a friendly receptionist writing on what looked like one of those marker boards you find outside restaurants advertising specials on the menu. "Hello, welcome to Friday!" she chirped as she walked me past a foosball table near the elevator and seated me by a fish tank. I filled out my "custom name tag" using scented markers, stickers, and little rubber animal stamps. The dress was casual and even a little sporty. At first I thought maybe I was in the wrong place, but I soon realized that my first impressions were a perfect reflection of the culture of this organization.

The Motley Fool was started by two brothers, David and Tom Gardner, in 1993 as a multimedia financial-services company that provides stock news and analysis and investment services. The company now manages a few mutual funds as well. It employs around 350 people (or "Fools") with a main office in Alexandria and smaller outposts all over the world. Leaders see the company as an alternative to Wall Street with core values that include collaboration, innovation, honesty, competitiveness, fun, and being "motley" (supporting employees' individual strengths and abilities). The Motley Fool was named the "Number 1 Medium-Sized Company to Work for in the United States" by Glassdoor.com in 2014 and 2015, and voluntary turnover rate is between 2 and 3 percent.

At the time the firm was founded, leadership decided employees would have unlimited vacation and holidays and could work wherever and whenever they needed to be effective. Employees are hired at The Fool because they are capable professionals who are trusted to deliver, with help from 360 peer reviews and results, not based on the number of hours they spend at the office. The company has a sizable coaching team, and each employee is provided with a coach who guides his or her career path and gives positive and constructive feedback, ensuring his or her success. Employees are moved around the organization frequently to expose them to different parts of the business but also to keep things interesting. In fact, employees are moved so much that all of the desks have legs with wheels so that people can quickly move from one team to the next.

Flexibility and being comfortable with change is apparently the name of the game.

The Motley Fool's chief wellness officer, Sam Whiteside, is separate from the human resources team (which is responsible for benefits and more traditional HR roles). Whiteside is responsible for designing the right mix of wellness challenge and exercise courses that will appeal to Fools, which she has learned through health screenings and assessments as well as one-on-one coaching. She teaches two to three classes daily for employees (like spinning, mixed martial arts, kettlebells, yoga, and boot camp), organizes the massage program, and selects the menu of free or subsidized healthy foods. She occasionally gives physical therapy in a pinch and orders custom ergonomic furniture like treadmill desks, sit-to-stand adjustable desks (for roughly 40 percent of the staff), and even wobble boards to stand on if employees request them. Some employees are uncomfortable with working out around coworkers, so Whiteside creates personal fitness programs for them to try at home. She even brings in puppies for employees to hold every once in a while to reduce the stress when employees have big deadlines.

Yes, The Motley Fool's office space operates as an office space. But just about every square inch is also used for other purposes. For example, hallways are perfectly good places for 4 p.m. plank competitions and sledge hammer workouts. Outdoor spaces, complete with fake grass and comfortable seating, are for eating, working, and happy hours. The Fool's large multipurpose space, sometimes used for lectures, panels, and events, can also be used as a gym. They move gym equipment on wheels in and out of closets to make the space more flexible. (See Figure 8-1.) There are also a number of team sports that happen nearby at a larger gym and on fields open to all employees, including soccer, hockey, and basketball, with games happening every day of the week.

The break area is stocked with healthy food like low-fat cheese, Greek yogurt, milk, and salads in refrigerators with

Figure 8-1. The Motley Fool's Wednesday kettlebell class in the company's multipurpose room. Image courtesy of Sam Whiteside.

glass doors, and nearby are shelves of bars, nuts, fruit, and other healthy snacks. Employees can preorder healthy meals and have them delivered to the office—Paleo, vegetarian, gluten-free, whatever their choice—and these are subsidized. Whiteside is still experimenting with the company's food provisioning, and she finds it is best to charge employees "just a little bit" for food items. When food was free, employees tended to take more than they needed and food would get wasted. By charging 25¢ or $1 for items, the refrigerator is less likely to "run out of milk by Wednesday," for example. Apparently, employees starting at The Fool used to regularly gain 15 pounds, but when CEO Tom Gardner found out about this, he was horrified. That is when more healthy food started appearing in break areas and more unhealthy foods, like sodas, disappeared from the office.

Participation in The Motley Fool's wellness program is at a record 90 percent (compared to a national average of 40 percent, according to Gallup), and it is clear that Whiteside, The Fool's leadership, and company investments in a highly customized and comprehensive program are a big part of the reason why.[5] But what is also clear is that the company is building a wellness program on top of a culture that is already highly supportive of autonomy and flexibility. This flexibility allows employees to take care of personal errands and family business, work out, or work at home if they choose, as long as they get their work done. One of their employees said it like this:

> We have a culture that allows us to work when and how we need to with not a lot of micromanagement. So when I want to get in a workout or participate in a soccer game or work at home one day for mental health, I just do it. I know what I need to get my work done, and I can easily fit workouts into my schedule. There is no cultural issue or penalty for participating in wellness activities. . . . I used to work for a large Fortune 100 company and they built a

beautiful workout facility. For the first six months it was packed, and you had to wait to use the treadmill. After that, though, people just stopped using it as much. I attribute that to the fact that the culture was not in support of people taking time to work out during the day.

A few of the employees I spoke with had lost quite a bit of weight during their time working for The Fool. I asked them if they felt as if their wellness program made a difference. They claim they made the decision to lose weight on their own and that it was a very personal decision to change their lifestyle. "But having coaching, a flexible work schedule, and a culture that embraces health made it much easier for me to integrate healthy behavior into my work and life," claims a woman who had started with The Fool 18 months earlier. She also says the company's wellness culture was one of the factors she considered before joining the company. "I get lots of encouragement here, which has really helped with my weight loss plan."

So how does The Motley Fool measure the ROI of its health and wellness investments? Leaders intentionally separated their wellness program participation and incentives from their health insurance program. They felt certain that employees would be less likely to participate in their program if they did. But they have noticed that it positively impacts employee recruitment and retention. For every job opening, they receive an average of 250 applicants. In addition, 84 percent of Fools say the wellness program is beneficial to them, making it one of the more popular benefits offered. Other than that, they know their investments in wellness impact the bottom line in other ways. One employee, who had lost 45 pounds and now coaches The Motley Fool soccer team, said, "I have more energy and I can sustain my work for longer periods of time, and I know this has made me a better employee." Another employee summed it up well: "We are our people. It's hard to imagine a better way to invest in the company. We realistically work anywhere from 8 to 11 hours a day. Make it convenient for employees to prioritize taking care of themselves and they will be able to give back more."

Again, health is not just tacked on to business as usual but integrated, and in fact, it is helped by The Motley Fool's culture. In addition to some great anecdotes, Sam Whiteside and the employees I met gave some good advice for other companies considering starting or expanding their health and wellness program.

■ Empower Your Employees

It's a lot to ask the leaders of organizations to come up with wellness programs that suit the personality and unique needs of their employee population. Leaders are charged with many things, first and foremost looking out for the financial well-being of the company, so coming up with new fitness incentive programs and food policies and deciding whether to buy treadmill desks is not the best use of their time or resources. Leaders should lay out a vision, but then they should empower smart and passionate people to help implement that vision. Besides, some of the most innovative health and wellness initiatives come from the ground up and from employees who are already interested in nutrition, fitness, or wellness.

To create internal champions for health at The Motley Fool, an employee is named the "Wellness Fool of the Month" and featured in the monthly wellness newsletter. Each Wellness Fool of the Month is then inducted into the Wellness Champions program for the next year. Wellness Champions help spread the word of wellness and all wellness offerings to their colleagues to drive participation in all aspects of the wellness program.

■ Keep the Channels of Communication Open

Give employees a voice when trying out new health and wellness initiatives. If they don't have someone to reach out and talk to, they can't give valuable feedback on what is working or not working. The Motley Fool uses Slack (as they call it, "the IM for 2015"), which has all kinds of ways that employees can connect to each other around different fitness, nutrition, or other health initiatives within the organization. They also provide wellness strategies for their external clients.

Whiteside creates a monthly challenge for The Motley Fool's clients (separate from the company's internal wellness program) with different health themes, and she made a series of videos for them highlighting exercises they can do along with other health advice.

■ Realize That It's a Work in Progress and You Have to Start Somewhere

A few years ago, Ben Sterling, one of The Motley Fool's employees who was a software engineer, was really into fitness and planned to leave the organization to become a personal trainer. He spoke with the company's leadership about it, and they asked, "Why don't you do that, but here?" Hence, the beginning of The Motley Fool's wellness program, when Sterling began offering a few classes during the day (outside of his regular job) to gauge interest. Sterling became the first Wellness Fool and eventually did break off to create his own personal training business; he is currently a contractor for The Motley Fool, working with remote and international employees on their wellness plans. The company now has a full-time chief wellness officer and a robust program, but this did not happen overnight. It was small to start and there were several rounds of fine-tuning along the way. Expecting programs to emerge as perfect right out of the gate is unrealistic.

■ Recognize That Wellness Is a Specialty and a Profession

It is often the case that corporate wellness is a responsibility that falls under human resources or environmental health and safety or possibly even under a local office manager. And for small organizations, this makes some sense because having someone fully dedicated to wellness could be too much of an expense. But at The Motley Fool and many other companies, wellness is emerging as a separate division or department altogether. Why? Because corporate wellness directors typically have a degree in health, fitness, nutrition, or mental health and their focus is solely on the mental and physical health of employees, as well as staying on top of the latest research, fitness, and health practices. It's a full-time job and then some. Sometimes companies choose to outsource this role, but to get the best outcomes, Sam Whiteside highly recommends bringing on an internal resource for supporting this function. She says:

> I used to work directly for a wellness consulting company and sat on-site as a fitness coach at an insurance company. Employees had a difficult time trusting me. They would ask, "How long are you going to be here?" They didn't think I would be around long enough or be vested in them to make a difference. It's much different working as a full-time employee. I'm treated as a colleague and "one of the guys." This has been essential for me to reach people who might not otherwise be engaged in a workplace wellness program.[6]

Even though Next Jump is considered a tech company and The Motley Fool a financial services company, what is abundantly clear is that each of them has a strong organizational culture of health. Both of these companies are about making money, and lots of it, but they see the physical, mental, emotional, and spiritual health of their employees and their stakeholder community as a part of a greater plan. Being healthy is not just a matter of doing a health assessment, slapping a few programs together, and buying some sit-to-stand desks. It is their competitive advantage, their engine, and why they are blowing their competition out of the water.

STRATEGIES THAT CHANGE BEHAVIOR

The magnetic pull of the couch is very strong. As mentioned in Chapter 4, performing regular exercise increases energy production, helps us feel more awake and alert, and creates endorphins that improve our spirits and mood. If we are exercising and moving around regularly, it is easy to keep doing so. But the opposite is true if we haven't been exercising and we've been sitting all day at work. We tend not to want to get up and move, and we are totally unmotivated. We need "nudges" to encourage us to change our behavior. We also need nudges to take health assessments, eat better, reduce stress during the day, and remind us to get some sleep. Many strategies that incorporate human psychology have been woven into the fabric of this book, but there are a few that have gotten more press lately than others and are worth mentioning.

■ Design Incentives for Desired Behaviors

Many workplace wellness programs provide financial incentives for things like getting health-risk assessments or biometric screenings, signing up for weight-management programs or meeting with a coach, meeting certain step counts, getting a flu shot, or signing up for races. Incentives might be in the form of money, gift cards, charitable contributions, or an increase in an employer's contribution to an individual health care premium. A number of companies are issuing employees pedometers or accelerometers (like a Fitbit, Jawbone, Nike Fuelband, or Basis) to help measure their daily steps as part of an incentive plan. The Vitality Group, a global organization that develops health promotion programs for hundreds of companies, measures wearable use and finds that individuals who do not ordinarily reach 5,000 or 10,000 steps a day will do so if given "points" as part of their plan.[7]

Experts generally agree that incentives work, but only if the program is designed well. For example, several years ago, General Electric partnered with Kevin Volpp at the University of Pennsylvania School of Medicine and Wharton School to test the effectiveness of using financial incentives as part of its smoking cessation program. Some employees were not offered a financial incentive (though they were given resources to quit), while others were offered a financial incentive of $100 for completing a smoking-cessation program, $250 for demonstrating (via a biochemical test) that they were cigarette-free after six months, and $400 for remaining cigarette-free for the following six months. Only those who quit in the first six months were eligible for the $400 bonus. The results of the study showed that three times as many people quit (15 percent versus 5 percent) when given financial incentives. Since smokers cost employers roughly $3400 more a year than nonsmokers, including added health care costs and lost productivity attributable to smoking, General Electric considered its financial incentives a good business move and went on to expand the program to all employees.[8]

Some companies have used employee incentives to advance social causes. In certain cases, helping others is more of a motivator than helping ourselves! In 2013, Microsoft and its employees joined forces with PATH (an international health organization) to help provide a vaccine to children in Asia through an innovative employee engagement campaign. Microsoft announced it would make a donation to support vaccine delivery for those in need for every employee who participated in its annual "Know Your Numbers" event providing free on-site health screenings. In addition, each participant could choose to donate an additional gift to PATH. More than 25,000 employees signed up for the screenings and participated in the campaign.[9]

■ Carefully Consider Disincentives

Some companies are not just rewarding good behavior—they are also penalizing employees who do not meet certain standards. A Towers Watson survey indicated that in 2015, 58 percent of U.S. employers rewarded or penalized employees based on tobacco use, a 38 percent increase over 2014 and twice the number doing so in 2011. Outside of tobacco use, 22 percent of employers in 2015 were using rewards and penalties to motivate employees to achieve certain biometric standards (e.g., weight control and cholesterol management), and more than twice as many (46 percent) expected to use them in 2016, nearly four times as many as used them in 2011.[10] Companies have gotten some serious pushback and negative press when using penalties, especially when employee performance is tied to denying health care benefits.[11] It is one thing if incentives or disincentives are in existence to nudge employees to make good choices, but it's another thing when employees not meeting health goals or refusing to participate in incentive plans results in their employer denying individual or family health care coverage. Some companies have chosen to completely untether their wellness incentives from their health care plans in order to increase participation in their wellness programs and keep incentives from feeling coercive.

■ Create a Buddy or Team System

Studies show that social influence or peer pressure has a positive impact on exercise behavior (both adherence and compliance), cognition of exercise involvement (both intention to exercise and to produce results), and attitudes associated with the exercise experience.[12] Tim Church of the Pennington Biomedical Research Center runs a consulting practice where he advises companies on how to create effective wellness programs. He finds that peer pressure in a work setting is important to making the program work. "A significant predictor of whether people are going to stay on an exercise program is if they have a friend (either an individual or group) who works out with them," he says. "Getting people connected to each other is critical."[13] We are hardwired not to want to let our friends down. We are social animals and if we promise someone we will meet him or her at the gym, we feel really guilty if we do not keep our promise.

▪ Leverage Gamification

Another powerful motivator to encourage people to move around more is to leverage *gamification,* the concept of applying video game thinking and game dynamics in a nongame context in order to engage people and change their behavior in some way. Commercial video games have been popular for years, and the gaming industry is one of the fastest growing industries in the world—proof that the products are desirable and highly addictive. Mike Tinney, a "gamer" in a previous life, has been studying aspects of social and behavioral engineering for online video games for years and is now applying them to games that encourage people to adopt more healthy behavior. His company, FIX: Fitness Interactive eXperience, and his games, UtiliFIT and A Step Ahead, integrate techniques like competition and progressive reinforcement, where a player gets a challenge, meets that challenge, and then receives an immediate reward for the accomplishment. Tinney reports that his top clients are seeing retained engagement as high as 90 percent from start to finish on their challenges. [14]

Jane McGonigal, a senior researcher at the Institute for the Future and the author of *Reality Is Broken: Why Games Make Us Better and How They Can Change the World,* has done a tremendous amount of research on what she calls "being gameful," which is using computer games of all kinds to minimize the negative impacts of posttraumatic stress disorder and depression, to improve happiness and resilience, and even to promote weight loss. In a trial with the University of Pennsylvania, study participants tested the benefits of using a game called SuperBetter, a Web-based and smartphone-based application that provides users with engaging, interactive content designed to help them achieve wellness goals. A version of the game was based on cognitive-behavioral therapy and positive psychotherapy and used with subjects suffering from depression. After just a month of daily use, the SuperBetter users' depression symptoms and anxiety decreased and life satisfaction and social support scores increased (based on survey data).[15]

Games like Candy Crush Saga, Bejeweled, and Tetris have been shown to reduce cravings for food, drugs, cigarettes, and other addictive habits by occupying the visual processing center of the brain, thereby reducing the vividness of naturally occurring cravings.[16] According to McGonigal, "A game like Candy Crush Saga can reduce cravings for things like food or cigarettes by 25 percent, which sounds like not a lot but it's actually been shown to be enough of a reduction of the craving that you can make a better choice and give your willpower a fighting chance."[17] It may be that playing video games, during a break time, can do more than relax employees: It can help them curb addictions too!

■ Provide On-Site Clinics or Coaches

Another effective trend in workplace wellness has been to bring the doctor's office to work. On-site health clinics give employees the opportunity to schedule visits for routine care without taking time off work. For smaller organizations that cannot offer this, consider having health coaches on-site in the workplace from time to time. Forty percent of U.S. companies now offer or are planning to offer a consumer-driven health plan that includes health coaching in some fashion.[18] It's one thing to talk generally about ways to be healthy at work—it's another thing to have one-on-one training with an expert who can show employees how to adjust behaviors at the worksite. Sometimes it's hard for people to visualize what being healthy looks like in their work setting, and consultants can be more helpful when they are convenient for employees and can make specific, customized recommendations.

The trick with using all of these behavior strategies at the organizational level is that (1) they do not always work for everyone, and (2) trying just one of them is not enough. Different individuals are motivated in different ways, as we all know. The best health and wellness plans are those that employ multiple interventions across all areas of health and with strategies to help individuals on their own, in teams, overtly, and more passively (like nice stairways or prominently displayed healthy food). The more integrated the approach, the better.

GETTING TO "WHY"

Becoming more healthy is a really good idea. But to get us to change our behavior—to actually change the way we eat, move, sleep, and manage our stress—requires a really powerful motivator. We need a reason that makes it absolutely essential for us to get off the couch and do things differently. Our lame excuses need to be trumped by a greater calling. We need a real sense of urgency and a strong "why."

This is where the Johnson & Johnson Human Performance Institute gives particular focus. People who are at the top of their game—athletes, Special Forces, CEOs—have a very strong reason for being their very best, mentally, emotionally, physically, and spiritually. They are not just healthy for the sake of being healthy. They are healthy because their job, their lives, or the lives of others depend upon it. During a session in my Corporate Athlete® course, my performance coach asked a really good question: "Imagine you are standing by a plate glass window on the 25th story of a building, and I told you that if you walked the long narrow plank between your building and the building next door, I would give you a million dollars. But what if I also told you that your chances for survival are pretty slim, because the wind might push you off balance, and the plank you will be walking on is fairly unstable. Would you walk the plank?" I like to think of myself as a bit of a risk taker, and a million dollars is a lot of money, but somehow I just could not see myself taking her up on an offer like that. Then she changed the scenario: "What if I told you that the building next door was actually on fire and that your children were in it? Would you walk the plank then?" My hand shot up. I have two little girls, and if they are in grave danger, you bet I would run across that plank, maybe even in high heels, to save them! And then, in a flash, I understood what she was really trying to say. Deciding to be healthy has to be more than just a cool thing to do or a "nice to have." Making the decision to change lifelong habits for the better requires steely resolve and a strong, unquestionable purpose. It has to be bullet-proof.

Having a purpose in mind—defining the reason "why" we should change our behavior—is essential to not just understanding the impact of our health issues but to actually doing something about it. Leaders have to have especially strong motivators, not only to inspire their own actions and set an example but to have the passion and drive to inspire others. As Golbie Kamarei says, "A strong 'why' can help navigate when the 'how' isn't so clear."[19]

At the organizational level, there are several strategies for why companies should rally behind supporting a healthy workforce and healthy workspace. But to get action, the case has to be really compelling, and the process for changing has to be sound. Take a minute to think about what it would take to give health a sense of urgency in your organization and what would help guide efforts as programs are implemented. Here are some thought starters.

■ Make a Good Business Case

What are some realistic catalysts for change? Is it the prospect of creating value for the company? Or is it the risks to the organization if it does not improve the health of its workforce? What is the appropriate case to be made that will best resonate with executives, managers, and employees? It is important to tie healthy initiatives to existing goals, priorities, or projects. Employee health and wellness is more likely to become a business imperative if it is tied to something precious to the organization. For example, for a hospital, health care company, healthy product company, or yoga studio, the idea of *not* doing everything to help the employees be their healthy best seems almost antithetical to the organizational mission and brand. Even if your organization doesn't have "health" in the name, there are likely goals related to people or performance that are easy to tie health to.

■ Make It Personal—Articulate the WIIFM

WIIFM is short for "what's in it for me." It is important to demonstrate to people why getting healthy benefits them personally and benefits the organization they work in too. It's all good to talk in broad terms, but taking things to an individual level, walking them through a typical day now and comparing it to changes they can make in the future, is a good way to make what you are suggesting come to life. Exactly how will healthy strategies support the individuals who work for you? How will their daily routines be changed? Will their families be affected? Will there be significant benefits that might not be obvious at first? Let's face it. Humans are naturally motivated by what is in their best interests, so engage people where they are, and help them take the next step in a way that makes sense for their unique situation.

I once met Ray Anderson, the founder and longtime CEO of

Interface, a carpet manufacturing company. Anderson transformed his business into one of the most environmentally sustainable companies on the planet. I asked him how he did it. "One mind at a time," was his simple response. He had spent his career convincing his employees to think about environmental sustainability in a different way, to convince them to help him build a sustainable company, and I think he was pretty insightful. I find that there is a similar challenge with health and wellness. Historically, companies have kept the personal lives and health of their employees at arm's length. Talking about health and its impact on company performance can feel a little intrusive, if not meddling. But it's really at the personal level, taking an interest in individuals and helping them to achieve personal health needs and goals, that minds are changed and results happen. Talking in generalities or creating high-level policies (without individual follow-up) just doesn't work all that well.

▪ Engage Employees Early and Often

If employees are involved, especially early on, they will be more likely to adopt new healthy strategies and to feel good about the process, their leadership, and the future of their organization. Involvement early on also ensures that strategies have been thought through fully from the start. When they hear this, most leaders get a little nervous. Isn't this a risky approach? I mean, why not just put a few smart people in a room to figure out what we're doing first, and then engage the rest of our staff in rolling out a program? The problem with this logic is that when employees aren't part of developing the strategy, they feel coerced and manipulated rather than excited and engaged. It ends up costing more in the long run if you wait to enroll people in the program. Engagement doesn't have to involve literally everyone in the organization, but it's important that all groups feel represented, which may mean engaging people in different departments and different offices, and from different age groups and even with different personalities (e.g., introverts versus extroverts).

Under Amour, Next Jump, The Motley Fool, and organizations with sustainable wellness programs check in with their employees on a regular basis through individual and small group coaching sessions throughout the year. They use real-time data from wearable devices, fitness tests, or just talking with their employees to find out how they are feeling about their health, their work, and their work environment to understand how it could be better. It may seem excessive, but many of the wellness experts and employees I spoke with believe wholeheartedly that health improvements and business outcomes can both be tied to having regular check-ins with employees. It's about good management.

■ Lead by Example

The biggest thing to take away about changing behavior in your organization is that it starts with you. Adopting healthy changes into your own life will give you the knowledge you need as a leader to convince others to change. If you take on eating better, moving more, focusing on your sleep, reducing stress, and rethinking your work patterns with health in mind, you are more likely to not only have more energy but also to understand the changes required to behave and work in a different way. You are also more likely to be listened to by the people you are trying to convince. It's really hard to take advice from someone who hasn't drunk the Kool-Aid themselves. I can't say it any plainer than that.

☯

Changing organizational culture requires leadership. Yours, and the leadership of many others, if you want to integrate the well-being of your employees into the way you do business. It takes research, collaboration, planning, testing and some time. The good news is that helping people improve their energy, decrease stress, and ease their work flow is generally a very positive message. It shows you care, even when you can't fund every project or idea.

The foundation for change is typically a campaign that crosses organizational boundaries and has short- and long-term goals and objectives. It fits into a wider business strategy and plan, not pasted on top of business-as-usual. The elements of this campaign are described in the next chapter.

The Business
Case for Health

G ALE TEDHAMS HAS BEEN WITH Owens Corning for
more than 30 years. She started in one of the product
divisions and is now director of sustainability, and she
has seen the company's focus on the environment and social
responsibility evolve over time. Owens Corning has been in
business since 1938, has about 15,000 employees in 26 countries, and has a workforce where 70 percent support manufacturing and the remaining support science and technology, sales
and marketing, and general corporate functions. It has been a
Fortune 500 company since 1952 and is likely the manufacturer
of many of the products in your home, including insulation,
roof shingles, and asphalt. Tedhams recalls a past CEO who
visited one of Owens Corning's suppliers at a mine several years
ago and was struck by how safe the working conditions were.
After that visit, he was convinced that "If the workers in that
mine could work in a safe environment, we all can." After that
point, Owens Corning put a significant focus on the safety of its
employees. Today, the company has excellent safety ratings,

with no fatalities for contractors and employees since 2006. It has started to look beyond injury rates and at leading indicators to injury, including first-aid cases or near misses, in order avoid issues before they occur.

In 2004, Owens Corning brought in a consultant who helped facilitate a workshop with roughly 40 people from across the company to assess how different parts of the organization addressed environmental, financial, health, and governance issues. At the time, the company was in bankruptcy due to financial liabilities associated with a former product that had contained asbestos. "This and the growing market demand for greener buildings were a catalyst for the company to really know our numbers around the environment and to have a robust product stewardship program," says Tedhams. "Social" factors like health and wellness were not a significant part of the business's corporate focus, with more attention being paid to environmental impacts and the product line. Owens Corning's first official sustainability report was published in 2007, and it has expanded every year to include new areas of focus. Later, they added sustainability metrics from their supply chain, and they continue to add other areas, including biodiversity and human rights. Today, the company is associated with organizations that continue to raise the bar, like the Dow Jones Sustainability Index, the Carbon Disclosure Project, and CERES's Global Reporting Initiative. Some of these organizations require a third-party audit, which helps to validate findings. Tedhams adds:

> Lately, we have started looking at our materials in a more rigorous way and also are paying attention to the engagement and well-being of our employees. For several years we have been doing health analytics, like screening for high blood pressure and cholesterol, as part of our health insurance benefits. Now we are thinking more about employee engagement. We want everyone to walk out of our

facilities in the evening and be in as good or better shape as when they came in. We see the value in keeping people happy and healthy.

Today, Owens Corning is one of the first companies to pilot Harvard's Health and Human Performance Index. This index measures employee well-being, productivity, engagement, and work culture and was developed by Harvard's School of Public Health in collaboration with Johnson & Johnson as a tool to enable more robust corporate sustainability reporting. "The initial results of this survey have set a baseline of data for us to measure again every 18 months to two years," Tedhams explains. "Even with the results of this first survey, however, we have learned things about our population that we were not aware of before, like the impact of mental health issues, the lack of sleep some of our employees are getting, and where smoking is more prevalent based on age." Especially across countries and regions, but also between the different functions in Owens Corning's workforce and between employees of different age groups, there are always unique health issues to be addressed. "Knowing the specific issues and what part of the employee population is most impacted is the first step to making things better."

Tedhams warns that all of this meeting, surveying, collecting data, and reporting is resource intensive. Owens Corning has a sustainability group dedicated to the work full time, but time is also borrowed across all functional and business areas, including human resources, operations management, community relations, and finance. If you count them all up, there are a sizable number of hours needed just to measure things like energy, carbon, water, and health outcomes, and training is continually required as people retire or move around in the organization.

As Owens Corning has rolled out its program globally, it has also learned the importance of working with local groups and the local culture. In some of its plants in China, workers are already doing tai chi every day, so wellness is more engrained. In those locations, health and wellness initiatives incorporate what is already there and build on it.[1]

THE ROLE OF COMMUNITY

Most organizations are aware that they do not operate in a vacuum. They are inextricably linked to their shareholders, their customers, and the communities where they operate. Company social responsibility and environmental-related reporting has become the norm, even an expectation, especially for large companies whose social or environmental impact is significant. And most companies didn't start doing this additional accounting on their own. Most have felt pressured or compelled to do it. Michael Porter and Mark Kramer, in a *Harvard Business Review* article in 2011, wrote, "The capitalist system is under siege. In recent years business increasingly has been viewed as a major cause of social, environmental, and economic problems. Companies are widely perceived to be prospering at the expense of the broader community."[2]

It is true that public goodwill has deteriorated for organizations operating in a bubble. But for smart organizations that understand the symbiotic relationship between their value and the value of the communities they serve, this connection is a competitive advantage. The more companies engage with their communities, the more successful they tend to be. Robert Eccles and colleagues at Harvard Business School report that companies with more community engagement significantly outperform their counterparts over the long term in terms of both stock market and accounting performance.[3] So the headline here is that companies that treat the community as a partner to help them achieve their goals are financially coming out ahead.

This synergy is particularly important to build upon when it comes to health, because companies are so heavily reliant on the community to build their workforce. According to a recent study from the Vitality Institute, major employment sectors with an unhealthy workforce are more likely to be located in counties with poor health.[4] If the community you operate in is unhealthy, regardless of how healthy your current employees might be, over time your organization will bear the cost. On the other hand, companies that take an active interest and invest in the health of their community are able to maintain and even improve the health of their workforce (while decreasing costs), increase retention, and increase the engagement of their employees. If companies are really savvy, they can also potentially tap into emerging market trends such as socially conscious or "net positive" products, services, or businesses. The Harvard School of Public Health's Sustainability and Health Initiative for NetPositive Enterprise (SHINE) is helping leading corporations across all sectors to measure and accelerate the ways in which they help the world become a healthier and more sustainable place. SHINE uniquely focuses not just on evaluating a company's "footprint" (or negative impact) but also on the corporate "handprint" (or positive impact) the company is making to the planet and human health. It is a powerful value proposition that is growing in popularity. Edelman, a global public relations firm, surveyed 8,000 consumers worldwide and found that 87 percent believe that businesses should place equal weight on industry and society, especially those in rapid-growth economies that have higher expectations of and engagement with brands on societal issues; 76 percent believe that it is all right for brands to support good causes and make money at the same time.[5]

Employers can invest in community health through strategic philanthropy or corporate social responsibility or by creating shared value, including extending their corporate health strategy. A great example of a company that applies each of these strategies is Whole Foods Market, a healthy supermarket chain. The company regularly reaches out to multiple stakeholders, including people who have an interest or an investment in what Whole Foods does or sells, such as customers, employees, suppliers, and investors as well as environmental and consumer groups who are watching out for how the company conducts its business. Whole Foods has had strong and steady financial success, partly because of good business decision making but also because of its commitment to the environment and engagement with the communities it serves. Individual stores have a lot of latitude in deciding the best way to operate and meet the needs of the local community, and community giving exceeds 5 percent of total net profits each year. Whole Foods Market has established independent nonprofit foundations to help with its efforts. One of them, Whole Planet Foundation, had as of late 2015 partnered with microfinance institutions to facilitate more than $67 million in grants to 116 projects in 69 countries where they source products. In addition, approximately 2,100 schools have received school garden grants and 3,500 have received salad bars through the Whole Kids Foundation and its partners. Whole Cities Foundation, founded in 2014, was put in place to improve individual and community health through collaborative partnerships, education, and broader access to nutritious food in underserved communities.

Whole Foods has continuously been ranked on Fortune's list of "the 100 Best Companies to Work for in America" for 17 years.[6] Even if you don't like their food or think it's too expensive, purely from a business perspective, you have to respect what they are doing. Their holistic, environmental, and community-based approach is working.

STRATEGIES FOR BUILDING A BUSINESS CASE

At this point, you hopefully have some ideas on healthy workplace strategies you would like to adopt, but maybe you need a little help getting started. I'm a firm believer in the power of a good business case. It can vary in length and complexity, of course, but the process of creating it has a great deal of value. In my experience rolling out new ways of working, process is just as important as the strategies ultimately adopted when it comes to making things happen. If you already have a wellness or health plan in place, build on that. But if your company is new to health and wellness, here are some suggestions.

■ Create a Wellness Vision and "Charter"

When organizing a wellness development team, many companies benefit from aligning expectations of leadership and employees, and establishing a project plan or charter. If you are creating a healthy wellness/workplace strategy for the first time or reenergizing your program to include some additional factors (like some of the elements listed in this book), it might be appropriate to do so. A charter can be formal or informal, but it is essentially a document that articulates the goals and objectives of the process, the roles and responsibilities of the development team, the expected outcomes of the process, and measures for success.

Creating a charter often starts with a vision session, similar to the work session Owens Corning had to reinvigorate its sustainability program. In this session, bring together key stakeholders to determine common goals and objectives. Because incorporating health and social responsibility into the workplace is a complex concept, many organizations ask consultants or other organizations to brief them on their experiences and lessons learned at this time. The vision should come from leaders and stakeholders and should reflect the values of the organization. Some probing questions to ask at this point might include:

▶ What areas are we doing well in and what areas require improvement to meet our healthy goals?

► How do our current business processes either enable or inhibit employees from becoming healthier?

► Is our business taking a holistic approach to health in the workplace, or are we just focusing on one area of our business?

The answers to these questions should be used to understand not only the current state of the organization but also the future desires of senior leaders and employees.

After the vision session, consider creating a plan that clearly defines sustainable principles in a larger context. The following are typically included in this plan:

► A list of key stakeholders including internal and external partners

► Background related to the project or initiative

► Anticipated benefits to the organization, the employees, and shareholders

► Benchmarks from other companies within and outside the company's industry

► Business need or justification for use of resources

► Criteria for success and measurement

► Risks, challenges, and constraints to achieving goals and measurements

► Schedule for completion including short- and long-term goals

► Deliverables or briefings to stakeholders

► Communication plan to employees and customers

► Roles and responsibilities of the sustainability team by region and by department

Creating a plan like this takes some work and coordination, but the benefits of creating it are significant. The plan outlines the business case for change, creates alignment and commitment across business sectors, and defines the resources needed internally and externally to bring the project (or series of projects) to fruition.

One of the more tricky steps at this point is assembling the team of people ultimately accountable for meeting comprehensive health and wellness goals. Should it be the health and wellness officer (a fairly new role for most organizations), the sustainability officer (health sometimes falls under social responsibility), human resources, or maybe environmental health and safety? Leading companies don't think of it that way. They consider employee health just like any other investment: Their employees are essential for their business to run well, and the more efficient and effective their employees are, the better they will perform. All areas of the organization are responsible for managing their people-investment, though what they are focused on might vary by function. Key groups worth including in your charter are, at a minimum, senior leadership, line management, environmental health and safety, human resources, IT, real estate and facilities, procurement, corporate communications, public relations, unions, community partners, and vendors (like food and beverage, insurance providers, or wellness consultants).

Set Health Targets, Tied to Third-Party Evaluation Tools

After a project charter and direction has been established, it's time to consider where you are starting from. At this point, measure the current state of your organization in order to assess the degree of change necessary. This may mean taking a step back and looking at your health and wellness strategy as part of a larger corporate social responsibility, human resources, or possibly even real estate strategy. This is a great time to reach out to a representative sample of people in the organization—to engage employees through screenings and health risk assessment surveys, focus groups, field observations, interviews, or by doing some benchmarking or researching best practices—to understand the current state of health in your organization. Health risk assessments and screenings are particularly important to understand the unique health risks of your organization and what your focus should be. This step is all about understanding the problems that need to be solved before the organization spends resources. It is also about collecting key performance metrics that are meaningful and lead to the right outcomes. Joseph Allen, with the Harvard School of Public Health, has started to use the term *health performance indicators* or HPIs (kind of like key performance indicators or KPIs) as the quantifiable measures of human health that can be used to identify drivers of negative and positive impacts of buildings on health, productivity, and the well-being of occupants.[7] More broadly, I think the term easily applies to non-building-related health indicators too.

So what are the right HPIs to focus on? As much as I would love to tell you, I'm afraid there is no core set of measures out there. For example, one recent study found that across six U.S. Health and Human Services measurement programs, there were 61 different measures for smoking cessation, 113 for HIV, 19 for obesity, and 68 for perinatal health.[8] Also, there are many health-related indexes, certifications, checklists, and third-party reporting systems out there, but nothing that is universally accepted and certainly nothing that is measured consistently on a global basis. And all of these different organizational health measures typically measure only pieces of the health or social responsibility picture within the organization. For example, some evaluate wellness programs (more typically managed by human resources or a wellness director); others are more focused on physical aspects of the workplace that improve occupant health (more typically managed by facilities management); others focus on the environment, with some human health factors thrown in (managed by a sustainability reporting team); and still others are about making sure products are designed or produced in a way that does not impact human health (work done by a product line or manufacturer).

Here is a list of some of the more popular health measures that is by no means comprehensive (note that the list is a bit U.S.-focused), but it gives a general sense of the landscape. It's worth exploring several different tools and seeing which ones best match your line of business. You may want to use more than one to suit your needs.

- American College of Occupational and Environmental Medicine's Corporate Health Achievement Award (CHAA)
- C. Everett Koop National Health Award, affiliated with the HERO Employee Health Management (EHM) Best Practices Scorecard
- Centers for Disease Control and Prevention's National Institute for Occupational Safety and Health (NIOSH) Total Worker Health program
- Partnership for Prevention's Leading by Example program (a communication campaign that educates CEOs about the benefits of worksite health promotion and encourages employers to adopt effective practices)
- Wellness Council of America (WELCOA) surveys and samples (a resource for building high-performing, healthy workplaces, including tools and methods for developing, delivering, and sustaining a healthy corporate culture)
- National Business Group on Health awards and benchmarking
- Baldrige Performance Excellence Program and Self-Assessment Tool from the National Institute of Standards and Technology (NIST)
- HealthLead Workplace Accreditation Program from US Healthiest
- Gallup-Healthways Well-Being Index
- Living Building Challenge and Red List (a list of "worst in class" materials, chemicals, and elements known to

pose serious risks to human health and the greater ecosystem)

▶ Leadership in Energy & Environmental Design (LEED) building certification

▶ Delos's WELL Building Standard and certification

▶ Center for Active Design's Guidelines

▶ Facility Innovations Toward Wellness Environment Leadership (FIT-WEL) certification

▶ Harvard School of Public Health's Health and Human Performance Index, which ties health to business performance indicators

The range of features highlighted or evaluated in some of these healthy workplace programs might include:

▶ HPIs such as well-being, weight management, smoking cessation, substance abuse, physical activity, healthy eating, blood pressure management, health care utilization/cost, absenteeism, disability, and safety incidents

▶ Data sources used to determine performance such as health risk assessment, medical claims data, and short-term disability claims

▶ If the standard is about a wellness program, questions about the program design, such as number of participants in the program, how groups or areas were selected, or current services provided such as immunizations, screenings, or counseling

▶ If the standard is about healthy buildings, questions about aspects of the workplace such as air quality, water quality, food quality, access to natural light, and amenities to encourage fitness, increase comfort, or decrease stress

▶ If the standard is about a healthy product, detailed questions about materials used and the manufacturing process

> How leadership, lines of business, employees, or the community are engaged in marketing campaigns, training, or the implementation of programs or strategies

> Outcomes achieved such as an increase in smoking cessation, number of pounds lost, reduced number of sick days, reduced cost of health care per person, increased number of steps taken per day and consistently good levels of air or water quality

> Statistics or analysis used to measure outcomes

> Innovations adopted to achieve outcomes

Collecting all of this information can be a giant task and one that requires full-time employees and/or the support of insurance companies, vendors, or contractors to collect. But at the end of the day, they are important to determine if your organizational health goals are met.

Calculate Your Wellness Program ROI

As mentioned in Chapter 1, in 2015, three researchers from Harvard University, Katherine Baicker, professor of health economics at the School of Public Health; David Cutler, professor of economics; and Zirui Song, a doctoral candidate at the Medical School, performed a meta-analysis, looking at the return on investment for 22 wellness programs. They looked at companies with a well-defined intervention, a well-defined treatment and comparison group—mostly larger companies with more than 1,000 employees—and a mix of financial services groups, manufacturing businesses, school districts, universities, and municipalities. As previously discussed, they found that medical costs fell by about $3.27 for every dollar spent on wellness programs and that absenteeism costs fell by about $2.73 for every dollar spent.[9] Compared to other similar studies, these findings are fairly conservative. Also, it's worth noting that roughly 30 percent of the companies in the study had incentive programs in place, and most of them focused on some combination of weight loss, fitness, smoking cessation, stress management, nutrition, alcohol consumption, and blood pressure.

If you are looking for individual case studies of companies that have engaged in fairly comprehensive studies of their health and wellness programs, check out Johnson & Johnson, which calculated a savings of $1.88 to $3.92 for every dollar spent on its program. In addition, Highmark Inc. saved $1.65 for every dollar spent on its program, and Citibank's return on investment was estimated to be between $4.56 and $4.73.[10]

The good news is that money spent on health and wellness programs seems to be paying off, but it's worth measuring these programs and their effectiveness to ensure they are working for your organization. The last thing you want to do is throw good money at strategies that don't really work or are half-baked. A great example of this is incentive programs. For every good incentive program, there are several others that fail because the reward is not closely correlated with the action they are intended to incent, they don't motivate employees, they are too prescriptive, or they encourage dishonesty.

▪ Consider the ROI for Other Health and Wellness Investments

Many of the ROI studies calculating the benefits of upgrades to the physical work environment are tied to biophilia, or the workplace providing access to natural light, views to nature, or elements that mimic nature. As previously discussed, there is mounting evidence that biophilic spaces can reduce hospital stays, reduce absenteeism, and increase productivity. Chapter 7 described an office building at the University of Oregon, where absenteeism was 19 percent higher for those with no view versus those with a view to nature, as well as a study by Roger Ulrich that showed that on average, patients recovering from surgery whose windows overlooked a scene of nature were released 9 percent sooner than patients whose views were of the hospital exterior walls.[11] In these cases and many others, the costs of making physical changes to the built environment pale in comparison to productivity costs.

In addition to a positive impact on building occupants, there is an inherent real estate value for buildings and workplaces that have access to water and/or views to nature. It's pretty clear when you look at property values. If your company is looking for a place for your workforce that will be easier to lease or sell later, consider moving to a building that has access or views to a park, green roof, lake, or other natural resource. In one study in Cleveland, Ohio, good landscaping aesthetics coupled with large shade trees added an average of 7 percent to rental rates, and housing with landscapes rated "excellent" were priced 4 to 5 percent higher than equivalent houses with poor landscaping.[12] In another analysis of condos and co-ops in Manhattan, Jonathan Miller, president and CEO of the appraisal firm Miller Samuel, found that apartments on floors with a view to a park or the East or Hudson rivers sold for roughly $100 square foot more than those on lower floors.[13]

Developers choosing to include healthy features like clean indoor air, day lighting, fitness centers, walking trails, open staircases, secure bike storage, healthy food options, and community spaces in their housing, mixed-use, and office buildings are seeing excellent returns on their investment. In a study by the Urban Land Institute, several developers of healthy building projects reported a market response that exceeded their expectations through rapid lease-up and sales rates, higher rents than pro forma projections, rent and sales premiums, waiting lists, and new interest by lenders and investors. There is a strong consensus that upfront development costs, even for those design features significantly more costly than standard approaches, were well worth the cost and contributed to the projects' overall success.[14]

■ Measure the Benefits of Health Investments to
   Recruitment and Retention

Findings from a recent survey by the Society for Human
Resource Management show that 45 percent of Americans
working at small to medium-size companies say that they would
stay at their jobs longer because of employer-sponsored wellness programs, according to their Principal Financial Well-
Being Index. The survey found that as a result of workplace
wellness programs, 40 percent of workers say they are encouraged to work harder and perform better and 26 percent miss
fewer days of work by participating in such programs.[15]

In many industries, health benefits and programs are more
than just nice-to-haves, they are essential. In the tech sector, the
average tenure for many companies today (including Amazon,
Google, eBay, and Apple) is less than 2 years.[16] Benefits consultant Towers Watson found in 2014 that technology and telecom
companies would pay an average $10,450 per employee for
health benefits that year, close to the top of the range, based on
a survey of expected expenses. The health care and energy sectors would both offer slightly more benefits, while wholesale
and retail employees would pay $8,162.[17] These are major costs,
but they are table stakes for some companies desperately trying
to recruit or keep top talent.

■ Evaluate the Impact of a Healthy Workplace on
   Organizational Performance

As mentioned in Chapter 1, some incredible work by Dr.
Raymond Fabius and his research team demonstrates that companies that have been recognized for their outstanding approaches to health and safety by the Corporate Health
Achievement Award (CHAA) outperformed the S&P 500 for
the 15-year period between 1997 and 2012, and in a separate
analysis over the 13-year period between 1999 and 2012. CHAA

winners had an annualized return for their portfolio between 3.03 and 5.27 percent compared to the S&P 500 annualized return of -0.06 percent.[18] According to Fabius: "Our results strongly support the view that focusing on the health and safety of a workforce is good business. Engaging in a comprehensive effort to promote wellness, reduce the health risks of a workforce, and mitigate the complications of chronic illness within these populations can produce remarkable impacts on health care costs, productivity, and performance."[19]

In case you are interested in which organizations have won the CHAA, take a look at American Express, Johnson & Johnson, the Smithsonian Institution, URS Corporation, Baptist Health of South Florida, and Southeastern Pennsylvania Transportation Authority (the winners since 2009). What's clear about these companies and other organizations that are seeing a positive return on their investments in employee health is that they are not making investments in a vacuum. They are looking at health measures and outcomes, incentives, and strategies that make sense for the culture and demographics of their workforce. They are customizing their solutions and improving them over time. You can find out what each of these companies did to win the award on the CHAA website, such as really creative strategies like American Express's "Healthy Living" mobile app and "Remote Site Ergonomic Evaluation Kit," which is shipped to employees who work virtually. The kit includes a webcam and measuring tape so ergonomists can see and evaluate virtual worksites.[20] The Smithsonian Institution— composed of nearly 10,000 employees, many of whom work across the world in remote areas—has developed robust training plans to help employees deal with a variety of injuries and communicable illnesses including zoonosis (any disease or infection that is naturally transmissible from vertebrate animals to humans and vice versa), pandemics, and animal escape drills (think the National Zoological Park).[21]

In my search for good benchmarks, stats, and quantifiable

data, I have discovered that it is clear that there are no hard and fast rules out there. Even the most progressive companies on the health and wellness front are experimenting with new ways to understand and tap into human performance. We know a great deal, but we have a long way to go. It seems the magic recipe for long-term success is *less* about what strategies the individual organization chooses and *more* about the fact that the organization has a culture that appreciates human health, a process in place that allows employees to test and adopt healthy strategies, and a way of measuring progress to know if they work.

THE FUTURE OF WORK

All good business cases include a little forecasting. But instead of straight-line financial projections or econometric modeling, this forecast is in story format, including two "future states" that take us several years from now out to the year 2025. One story is about the status quo, or business as usual, while the second involves some intervention. Both are based on current trends but describe very different outcomes.

■ Story 1: Business as Usual

In the first scenario, imagine things continue along the path they are today. Our work for the past 50 years has gradually become more sedentary, and this continues on, so that we are spending fewer calories on a daily basis.[22] We are spending more time than ever at work staring at screens: PCs, tablets, phones, or other devices. Our daily average caloric intake exceeds caloric burn by 190 kcals for men and 160 kcals for women because we are sedentary (assuming we are eating the same amount in 2025 as we are in 2015 and current sedentary trends continue).

We also continue to eat more processed foods. Companies do not put pressure on food service vendors to provide better-quality food options because vendors have figured out what people eat and what makes money—no reason to get in the way of that. Besides, asking people to eat differently might cause worse headaches than asking vendors to change, like dealing with pushback from employees. We know from vending machine companies that people really like their Snickers, Doritos Big Grab, Peanut M&Ms, Cheetos, Cheez-Its, Twix bars, Strawberry Frosted Pop-Tarts, Rice Krispies Treats, Lay's Chips, and Mrs. Freshley's Jumbo Honey Buns![23] Asking employees to eat chia, fruit, and microgreens would probably cause rioting in the streets. It's really best to keep things as they are. But is it?

Keeping things status quo means the intake of processed foods and lack of movement for many workers continues to increase obesity levels to record highs. According to the Centers for Disease Control, the average American in 2010 was more than 24 pounds heavier than in 1960.[24] Two-thirds of Americans are overweight, and one-third are obese. Sadly, the rest of the planet is not far behind. As the rate of obesity continues to grow, the impact becomes even more devastating for business. This is primarily because health care costs rise, so much so that many companies can no longer afford to subsidize insurance for their employees at the rate they do today. They must either rely on a variable or part-time workforce, or they continue to pay health insurance but reduce worker salaries to be able to compete globally. Increased obesity levels also increase levels of absenteeism, with many workers taking extended time off to deal with chronic diseases, their own or that of members of their families.

The "Internet of Things" (the network of physical objects embedded with electronics, software, sensors, and network connectivity that collect and exchange data) tracks everything as a means to control health care costs. If employees buy healthy food at the grocery store, they are rewarded, but they are penalized when they purchase unhealthy processed food.

Employees are measured by whether they get regular flu shots, take 10,000 steps daily, or perform tasks that do not support good ergonomics. Though all of these systems and wearables are good for health, they become more and more invasive, so that employees begin to resent them and disengage.

Email continues to be the communication tool of choice, closely followed by instant messaging, social media, and new project management tools. More than ever, employees are on-call all the time and working more at home, on trains, on planes, and in automobiles. As a result, they continue to depend on these electronic "different time, different place" collaboration tools to communicate, versus phone calls or meeting face-to-face. Because these tools are so easy to use asynchronously, businesses now expect employees to be available at all times of the day or night. In 2015 this is an issue for some, but in 2025 it is a mandate for everyone. Working all the time increases stress, which impacts presenteeism and absenteeism. Workers feel they need to take even more mental health days away from work to deal with the constant pressure to keep up.

Increased levels of obesity and stress negatively impact employees' sleep, the foundation of health that should help reset their minds and bodies each night. With less sleep, employees gain even more weight, their stress levels increase, and many more are subject to sleep disorders, which all put them at risk for problems like addictions to sleeping pills or sleep apnea.

The physical work environment is now all about efficiency and saving money. According to the Brookings Institution, the United States will need to build roughly 100 billion square feet of commercial and industrial space between now and 2030 to accommodate business and economic growth projections. Even with reduced demand for new workspace due to the large numbers of people working from home, this is still a significant amount of new construction.[25] To keep costs down, workplaces become even more open, denser, and generally more stressful. Sure, the sustainability trend and cities with greenscapes are getting the media buzz now, but this eventually dies off as populations grow, cities become more and more compact, and environmentally friendly buildings and urban environments are a political hot potato. As much as people enjoy plants, landscapes, and natural light, these are "nice-to-haves" and not considered essential given other priorities for funding. The federal government and some cities require LEED certification for their buildings today, but in the near future these green and healthy buildings are dwarfed by the number of private organizations developing, designing, and constructing more modest investments to house their growing businesses. Because health care is such a crushing expense, there is less money left over for creating for green space, landscaping, or places of psychological restoration.

This status quo scenario is really not so hard to imagine. All of the events described here are not that far away, and they are slowly creeping up on us. We are like frogs in a pot of hot water. If you throw frogs in a pot of hot water, they jump right out, but if you put them in a pot of cool water and slowly increase the temperature, they don't feel it and eventually boil to death. Not a pleasant thought! But what is the alternative? How might we imagine a future that is healthier—for people, for communities, and for business? What does that look like?

■ Story 2: The Workplace Evolves

In this alternative future, let's imagine that the world takes note of the health crisis and businesses, along with governments, NGOs, and universities, all make human health the foundation of an international campaign. The motivations of each of these groups are at the same time altruistic and selfish: They want better health, but they also see tremendous business and economic opportunities in addressing health issues and doing so holistically. Smart companies work with partners that can help them improve health in the regions where they do business.

Their strategies are customized to incentivize and address the specific issues of their employee population and that of the local community.

Innovation districts, those geographic areas where leading-edge anchor institutions and companies cluster and connect with start-ups, business incubators, and accelerators, continue to evolve, and they put health front and center. Whether it's through innovations in life sciences, material sciences, nanotechnology, social media, small-scale manufacturing, industrial design, graphic arts, media, architecture, or a growing number of hybrid industries, these innovation hubs become production centers for cutting-edge technologies, products, and services. They are physical examples of places that promote healthy living, but also spawn new health-related business ideas and spur economic growth.[26] These emerging businesses use wearables, devices, and systems that help patients spend less time in the hospital and more time at home recovering. They also help employees better manage their health and prevent health problems to begin with, and in ways that individuals can control and monitor on their own.

The hospitality industry continues to promote and benefit from wellness tourism, which is travel for the purpose of promoting health and well-being through physical, psychological, or spiritual activities. Currently, wellness tourism accounts for 15 percent of all U.S. domestic and international tourism, with annual expenditures of $500 billion. This industry, as well as consumer health in general, meets estimated targets and grows by almost 50 percent over the next five years.[27] Travelers for business or pleasure can expect to have tailor-made meals to support dietary restrictions, a personal trainer, or a sleep specialist available to them to ensure their stay is comfortable and productive.

There is a war for talent happening between cities and states everywhere. In order to compete, mayors and governors are rethinking ways to enhance rooftops, old train tracks, roads, and bridges, to make them more livable with trees, greenhouses, urban farms, and lush landscapes for residents. Real estate developers take sustainable and healthy buildings to the next level. To compete for tenants, they retrofit and build structures that are net energy positive (create more energy than they use) through renewable energy sources on-site (like solar, geothermal, and wind). These new buildings not only prevent pollution but actually clean the air. Some of the new energy solutions include covering buildings in green walls including algae tubes, which feed on carbon dioxide while providing energy to the building.[28]

Finally, the $500 million commitment from the Robert Wood Johnson Foundation to reduce childhood obesity has placed the needs of our future workforce center stage. Researchers, professional groups, and government agencies team to understand and incentivize children and young adults so that eating nutritious foods and working out is part of our global youth culture. It keeps our teachers healthy, too.

Though the first scenario presented here paints a doom and gloom picture and the second scenario is probably overly optimistic, both illustrate possible futures. They are based on trends and major movements already happening around the world. The big difference between these two outcomes will be our shift in mindset and focus. As business leaders, it's easy to get buried in quarterly returns, overhead costs, and the challenges of day-to-day business, and to miss the elephant in the room. Health is clearly going to be a major impact over the next decade and beyond. The question is, will it be a cost or an opportunity? Will it feed or hinder our global economy? I chose to think optimistically, to image infinite business opportunities for addressing health and fueling a productive workforce of the future. Naive? I don't think so. It's just called working *smarter*.

Afterword

THE FOLLOWING TABLE IS A summary of many of the strategies shared in this book. Think of it as your cheat sheet. Each strategy has been classified into three general categories: (1) They are marked "X" if they involve creating a new policy or business process, (2) they are marked "X" if they require the adoption of new technology, buying new furniture, or changing the physical workplace/facility in some way, and (3) they have been given a ranking of 1 to 3 based on the degree of difficulty in implementation. Of course, depending on the culture or various constraints in your organization, the level of difficulty may vary. This just gives you a general sense of the typical level of effort.

HEALTHY WORKPLACE STRATEGIES	POLICY OR BUSINESS PROCESS	TECHNOLOGY, FURNITURE, OR FACILITY	LEVEL OF DIFFICULTY (1=EASY, 3=DIFFICULT)
INCREASE MOVEMENT			
Use "point of decision" prompts to encourage stair use	X		1
Encourage employees to stand up	X	X	1
Double up workspace for exercise or stretching	X	X	1
Encourage and enable employees to walk	X	X	1–2
Make stairs more attractive to use		X	2
Carve out space for bikes or showers		X	2
Locate your office space by public transportation or amenities		X	3
Provide a place for employees to work out		X	3
IMPROVE NUTRITION			
Provide a place for employees to eat their lunch	X	X	1–2
Provide healthy, portioned meals or snacks for employees	X		2
Make healthy choices the default setting	X	X	2
Leverage healthy catering and vending options	X		2
Provide places for employees to grow their own food	X	X	3

HEALTHY WORKPLACE STRATEGIES	POLICY OR BUSINESS PROCESS	TECHNOLOGY, FURNITURE, OR FACILITY	LEVEL OF DIFFICULTY (1=EASY, 3=DIFFICULT)
REDUCE STRESS			
Provide choice as to when employees can work	X		1
Encourage employees to take their vacation	X		1
Allow employees to bring their pets to work	X		1
Allow employees to bring their children to work	X	X	1
Allow employees to choose how they work	X		1–2
Develop a stress management program	X		2
Encourage employees to focus on one task at a time	X		2
Get rid of email (or change how you use it)	X	X	2
Provide choice for where employees can work	X	X	2
Design places for psychological restoration	X	X	2–3
IMPROVE SLEEP			
Encourage employees to go outside, especially early in the day	X		1
Encourage employees to exercise during the day	X	X	1
Set devices to change light levels over the course of the workday	X	X	1
Cut out caffeine service by late afternoon	X		1

HEALTHY WORKPLACE STRATEGIES	POLICY OR BUSINESS PROCESS	TECHNOLOGY, FURNITURE, OR FACILITY	LEVEL OF DIFFICULTY (1=EASY, 3=DIFFICULT)
Set the example and/or set a policy for employees to unplug	X		1
Give employees time to sleep through tough work problems	X		1
Encourage employees to use hotels that better cater to their sleep and health on the road	X		1
Accommodate your workforce by a window		X	2
Install circadian lighting		X	2
Provide napping or wellness rooms		X	3
IMPROVE SLEEP FOR SHIFT WORKERS			
Keep the workplace well lit with bright lights to promote alertness		X	1
Encourage employees to be active during breaks	X		1
Do not assign tedious or boring tasks at the end of shifts	X		1
Do not schedule workers for a number of night shifts in a row	X		2
Avoid scheduling frequently rotating shifts	X		2
Provide night shift workers with amber glasses when leaving work in early daylight		X	1
Create a work environment where employees work together to help them stay alert		X	3
CREATE A HEALTHY WORK ENVIRONMENT			
Keep the workplace tidy	X		1

HEALTHY WORKPLACE STRATEGIES	POLICY OR BUSINESS PROCESS	TECHNOLOGY, FURNITURE, OR FACILITY	LEVEL OF DIFFICULTY (1=EASY, 3=DIFFICULT)
Train employees how to set up their work point to minimize muscle strain	X		1
Create policies for removing distracting behaviors in the workplace	X		1
Encourage employees to stay at home when they are sick	X		1
Use smell to increase productivity	X		1
Integrate plants and views to nature into the work environment	X	X	1–2
Maximize natural light in the workspace		X	2
Upgrade furniture and finishes		X	2
Use color strategically		X	2
Choose workplaces with volume		X	3
Consider wall construction, materials, and height		X	3
Improve thermal comfort and air quality		X	3
ADOPT STRATEGIES TO CHANGE BEHAVIOR			
Create a fitness challenge	X		1
Leverage gamification	X	X	1
Design incentives and disincentives	X		2
Create a buddy or team system	X		2
Provide on-site clinics or coaches	X	X	2

HEALTHY WORKPLACE STRATEGIES	POLICY OR BUSINESS PROCESS	TECHNOLOGY, FURNITURE, OR FACILITY	LEVEL OF DIFFICULTY (1=EASY, 3=DIFFICULT)
CREATE A BUSINESS CASE FOR CHANGE			
Create a wellness vision and charter	X		1
Set health targets, tied to third-party evaluation tools	X		1
Calculate your wellness program ROI	X		2
Consider the ROI of other health- and well-being-related investments	X		2
Measure the benefits of heath investments for recruitment and retention	X		2
Evaluate the impact of a healthy workplace on organizational performance	X		2

ACKNOWLEDGMENTS

IT WOULD NOT HAVE BEEN possible for me to write this book without the encouragement and support of my husband, John Hlinko, and my parents, Jim and Mary Helen Stringer. I am also extremely grateful to my employer, EYP, for being flexible and giving me the space to write. Their flexibility speaks volumes. A big thank you to Teresa Rainey, Director of High Performance Design at EYP; Robyn Baxter, Regional Leader of Consulting for HOK Canada; Lauren Abramo, my agent; my editor, Stephen S. Power and the many editors and staff who helped me shape and craft this book.

The process of writing this story, about health at work, has been about discovery. None of us really has this health thing figured out—or we would not have the problems we have today—but there are some real champions for health and wellness in our midst who graciously agreed to speak with me and offer what they have learned. I would like to thank and acknowledge the researchers and health professionals at the Pennington Biomedical Research Center in Baton Rouge, Louisiana, especially Tim Church, MD, MPH, PhD, professor of preventative medicine; Peter Katzmarzyk, PhD, FACSM, FAHA, professor and chair of pediatric obesity and diabetes, associate executive director of population and public health sciences; and Amanda Staiano, PhD, assistant professor of research. Thank you as well to Catrine Tudor-Locke, PhD,

FACSM, professor and department chair of kinesiology at the University of Massachusetts, Amherst.

I would like to thank and give a big virtual hug to the people and my performance coaches at the Johnson & Johnson Human Performance Institute (JJHPI) in Orlando, Florida. They helped shape some of the content of this book, but more importantly, they helped me to define my ultimate purpose and how my personal health goals fit into my life as a whole. Their Corporate Athlete® program is outstanding and I would recommend it to anyone. In particular, a big thank you to Bill Donovan, general manager of JJHPI, and Brett Klika, Chris Mohr, PhD, RD, and Rhonda Waters, MEd, my performance coaches and advisers.

A very special thank you to my colleagues and partners in crime at the Center for Active Design: Joanna Frank, executive director, Suzanne Nienaber, partnerships director, and all of the amazing health and design experts on the health and well-being committee. And thank you to Eileen McNeely, PhD, MS, RNC, co-director, SHINE, Center for Health and the Global Environment, Harvard School of Public Health, and to Ron Goetzel, PhD, senior scientist at Johns Hopkins Bloomberg School of Public Health. Their work is foundational for making the business case for health today.

Several people recommended that I go to Miraval, a health and wellness resort in Tucson, Arizona. If you have ever been there, you know that it is a real treat. Many people visit when they are grieving or dealing with health or relationship issues. I visited because I was exhausted from work and felt it might be a good place for recovery. It turns out this is true: Miraval is a wonderful place for quiet, serenity, a few choice spa treatments, and workshops to improve physical, mental, and spiritual well-being. I'm particularly grateful for my instructors, Sheryl Brooks, RN, a certified health coach who first introduced me to the issue of sleep apnea (which my husband was diagnosed with shortly afterward); Anne Parker, MA, wellness counselor; Andrew Wolf, MEd, RCEP, exercise physiologist; Wyatt Webb, creator of the Miraval Equine Experience; and Junelle Lupiani, RD, nutritionist (now with Green Mountain at Fox Run).

I highly recommend visiting the Human Origins Exhibit at the Smithsonian's National Museum of Natural History in Washington, DC. I took an outstanding tour there and got some great advice during my paleo research adventure from Briana Pobiner, PhD, research scientist and museum educator, Human Origins Program, Department of Anthropology. She and many of her colleagues put together an amazing exhibit.

I'm very "mindful" of Joy Rains, meditation speaker, author, and guide, who taught me how the workplace can be a great place for mindfulness, and to David Gelles, author of *Mindful Work*, who nudged me to attend Wisdom 2.0 Business, a conference in New York about meditation and mindfulness for business leaders. A big thanks to Brigid Schulte, whose book *Overwhelmed: Work, Love, and Play When No One Has the Time* and advice kept me from being "overwhelmed."

I had the great pleasure of speaking to several specialists and experts in their field, in addition to the ones I have already mentioned, who were invaluable to my full understanding of many of the issues addressed in this book. They include Sara Crain, physical therapist and ergonomics specialist at Mercy Hospital; Nancy H. Rothstein, The Sleep Ambassador; Alan Pollard, CEO, Vitality Group; Mike Tinney, CEO, FIX: Fitness Interactive eXperience; Shir Nir, CEO, the Handel Group; and David Conrath, with Anthrospheres.

And finally, I'd like to thank people from the many "healthy" organizations who took time to speak with me and to share their stories and insights. You all were invaluable to me as resources for understanding employee health from an employer perspective, and you have demonstrated how employers can make a difference in the lives of their people. Thanks especially to Peter Chiarchiaro, head of wellness at Next Jump; Sarah Kalamchi, environment specialist with Tilt.com; Sam Whiteside,

209

chief wellness officer, David Meier, Jill Ralph, Megan Brinsfield, and Michael Douglass at The Motley Fool; Newton Cheng, fitness programs manager, Google; Nate Costa, FX Studios and Under Armour Performance Center; April Floyd, global benefits, Under Armour; Mark Cunningham-Hill, MD, director, Global Solutions Center, and head of occupational medicine for Johnson & Johnson; Deb Gorhan, wellness and health promotion manager Americas, for Johnson & Johnson; Megan Benedict, global health and vitality manager at IBM; Meg Bach, U.S. health promotion operations lead at IBM; Gale Tedhams, director of sustainability for Owens Corning; and David Ribble, professor of biology at Trinity University.

You are each an inspiration.

SUGGESTED READING

THERE ARE A WEALTH OF fantastic books that elaborate on the themes and ideas mentioned in this book. There are powerful statistics, stories, and messages in each of the following, so they are on my suggested reading list. For the latest articles and research on health and well-being, see the Notes in this book, or go to LeighStringer.com.

WELL-BEING AND HEALTH

Healthy Work: Stress, Productivity, and the Reconstruction of Working Life by Robert Karasek and Tores Theorell (Basic Books, 1990).

Overwhelmed: Work, Love, and Play When No One Has the Time by Brigid Schulte (Sarah Crichton Books, 2014).

The Corporate Athlete Advantage: The Science of Deepening Engagement by Jim Loehr (Human Performance Institute, 2008).

Thrive: The Third Metric to Redefining Success and Creating a Life of Well-Being, Wisdom, and Wonder by Arianna Huffington (Harmony, 2014).

Well-Being: The Five Essential Elements by Tom Rath and James K. Harter (Gallup Press, 2010).

MINDFULNESS

10% Happier: How I Tamed the Voice in My Head, Reduced Stress Without Losing My Edge, and Found Self-Help That Actually Works—A True Story by Dan Harris (It Books, 2014).

Meditation Illuminated: Simple Ways to Manage Your Busy Mind by Joy Rains (Whole Earth Press, 2013).

Mindful Work: How Meditation Is Changing Business from the Inside Out by David Gelles (Eamon Dolan/Houghton Mifflin Harcourt, 2015).

Mindless Eating: Why We Eat More Than We Think by Brian Wansink (Bantam, 2007).

HUMAN EVOLUTION

Paleofantasy: What Evolution Really Tells Us about Sex, Diet, and How We Live by Marlene Zuk (Norton, 2013).

Sapiens: A Brief History of Humankind by Yuval Noah Harari (Harper, 2015)

What Does It Mean to Be Human? by Richard Potts and Christopher Sloan (National Geographic, 2010).

FLOW AND CREATIVITY

Flow: The Psychology of Optimal Experience by Mihaly Csikszentmihalyi (Harper Perennial Modern Classics, 2008).

Group Genius: The Creative Power of Collaboration by Keith Sawyer (Basic Books, 2008).

Imagine: How Creativity Works by Jonah Lehrer (Houghton Mifflin, 2012)

The Rise of Superman: Decoding the Science of Ultimate Human Performance by Steven Kotler (New Harvest, 2014).

Where Good Ideas Come From: The Natural History of Innovation by Steven Johnson (Riverhead Books, 2010).

HEALTHY ENVIRONMENT

Biophilic Design: The Theory, Science, and Practice of Bringing Buildings to Life by Stephen R. Kellert, Judith H. Heerwagen, and Martin L. Mador (Wiley, 2008).

Place Advantage: Applied Psychology for Interior Architecture by Sally Augustin (Wiley, 2009).

NOTES

PREFACE

1. For the record, I really enjoyed Sheryl Sandberg's book *Lean In: Women, Work, and the Will to Lead*, mostly because she challenges women to rethink stereotypes and the constraints they put on themselves. It's worth reading her book and hearing her out. I do not recommend reading this book when you have not been sleeping for months, however! Bad idea.

2. The U.S. Department of Health and Human Services advises that adults do at least 150 minutes per week of moderate intensity physical activity, or 75 minutes per week of vigorous aerobic exercise. The American College of Sports Medicine, American Heart Association, and World Health Organization state similar guidelines, advocating that adults under the age of 65 should have at least 150 minutes of moderate intensity activity per week (30 minutes, five times per week), or 60 minutes of vigorous intensity aerobic activity (20 minutes, three times per week). In its most recent dietary guidelines, the Institute of Medicine sets the bar a bit higher, recommending one hour per day of moderate intensity exercise.

3. R.P. Troiano, D. Berrigan, K.W. Dodd, L.C. Masse, T. Tilert, et al., "Physical Activity in the United States Measured by Accelerometer," *Med Sci Sports Exerc*, 2008, 40: pp. 181–188.

4. Jonah Lehrer, "How to Be Creative," *Wall Street Journal*, March 12, 2012.

5. Ewa Hudson, "Health and Wellness the Trillion Dollar Industry in 2017: Key Research Highlights," *Euromonitor International*, November 19, 2012.

6. Tim Ferriss, author of *The 4-Hour Body*, is, according to *Wired* magazine, a self-made lab rat. He regularly subjects himself to experiments in physical training and nutrition in order to test new ideas in the field. He has a particularly good podcast, The Tim Ferriss Show, which I highly recommend.

CHAPTER 1

1. A plethysmograph is an instrument for measuring changes in volume within an organ or whole body (usually resulting from fluctuations in the amount of blood or the air it contains).

2. The Corporate Athlete® course does not use or provide these particular BODPOD® data, though many physical trainers use them.

3. I attended a Corporate Athlete® course in July 2014. I reference my

experience there in Chapters 1, 4, and 8. The people taking my class included leaders from organizations across the globe and the performance "coaches" for my course included Brett Klika, Chris Mohr, PhD, RD, and Rhonda Waters, MEd.

4. Shawn T. Mason et al., "The Life Benefits of Managing Energy," Johnson & Johnson Human Performance Institute white paper, 2015. JJHPI used the SF-36 to survey participants before they participated in the Corporate Athlete® course and again in 6, 12, and 18 months. Outcomes are based on aggregate scores from eight separate subscales calculated from participant responses.

5. Ibid. Productivity outcomes were based on the Work Productivity and Activity Impairment (WPAI) questionnaire. The WPAI is a self-report tool designed to assess productivity impairment.

6. J. Brandon, R. Joines, T. Powell, S. Cruse, and C. Kononenko, "Developing Fully Engaged Leaders That Bring Out the Best in Their Teams at GlaxoSmithKline," *Online Journal of International Case Analysis*, 2013, 3(2). Retrieved from ojica.fiu.edu/index.php/ojica_journal/article/view/63/45.

7. Centers for Medicare & Medicaid Services, "National Health Expenditure Data." Available at www.cms. gov/Research-Statistics-Data-and-Systems/Statistics-Trends-and-Reports/NationalHealthExpendData/NationalHealthAccountsHistorical.html. Accessed May 23, 2015.

8. J. Gerteis, D. Izrael, D. Deitz, et al., "Multiple Chronic Conditions Chartbook," Agency for Healthcare Research and Quality, 2014. Available atahrq.gov/professionals/prevention-chronic-care/decision/mcc/mccchartbook.pdf. Accessed May 25, 2015.

9. Employee Benefit Research Institute, *EBRI Databook on Employee Benefits.* Updated July 2014. www.ebri.org/pdf/publications/books/databook/db.chapter%2002.pdf. Accessed March 12, 2015.

10. D.E. Bloom, E.T. Cafiero, E. Jané-Llopis, et al., *The Global Economic Burden of Noncommunicable Diseases.* World Economic Forum, 2011.

11. Fryar, Cheryl D. M.S.P.H.; Margaret D. Carroll, M.S.P.H.; and Cynthia L. Ogden, Ph.D., "Division of Health and Nutrition Examination Surveys, Prevalence of Overweight, Obesity, and Extreme Obesity Among Adults: United States, 1960–1962 Through 2011–2012", CDC National Center for Health Statistics, September 2014.

12. www.oecd.org/health/healthdata.

13. W.F. Stewart, J.A. Ricci, E. Chee, and D. Morganstein, "Lost Productive Work Time Costs from Health Conditions in the United States: Results from the American Productivity Audit," *Journal of Occupational and Environ Medicine*, 2003, 45(12): pp. 1234–1246.

14. E.A. Finkelstein, I.C. Fiebelkorn, and G. Wang, "The Costs of Obesity Among Full-Time Employees," *Am J Health Promot*, 2005, 20(1): pp. 45–51.

15. NIH, NHLBI Obesity Education Initiative, *Clinical Guidelines on the Identification, Evaluation, and Treatment of Overweight and Obesity in Adults.* Available at www.nhlbi.nih.gov/guidelines/obesity/ob_gdlns.pdf.

16. World Health Organization, *WHO Report on the Global Tobacco Epidemic, 2011.* World Health Organization, 2011. Accessed April 7, 2015.

17. www.cdc.gov/mmwr/pdf/wk/mm6035.pdf#page=21.

18. *The Burden of Musculoskeletal Diseases in the United States*, second edition, 2011. Available at www.boneandjointburden.org/pdfs.

19. www.hse.gov.uk/statistics/causdis/musculoskeletal/.

20. A.E. Staiano, D.M. Harrington, T.V. Barreira, et al., "Sitting time and cardiometabolic risk in US adults: associations by sex, race, socioeconomic status and activity level," *Br J Sports Med*, 2014, 48: pp. 213–219; Bridget Healy, Erik Levin, Kyle Perrin, Mark Weatherall, and Richard Beasley, "Prolonged Work- and Computer-Related Seated Immobility and Risk of Venous Thromboembolism," *Journal of the Royal Society of Medicine*, 2010, 103: pp. 447–454.

21. *Stress in America*, American Psychological Association, February 11, 2014.

22. Stewart et al., "Lost Productive Work Time Costs." Other studies show the costs of presenteeism to be much, much higher, some as high as $300 billion; this source is fairly conservative.

23. Ronald Loeppke et al., "Health and Productivity as a Business Strategy: A Multiemployer Study," *Journal of Occupational and Environmental Medicine*, April 2009, 51(4).

24. C.E. Matthews, K.Y. Chen, P.S. Freedson, et al., "Amount of Time Spent in Sedentary Behaviors in the United States, 2003–2004," *Am J Epidemiol*, 2008, 167(7): pp. 875–881.

25. io9.com/5988852/ an-interactive-map-of-average-us-commute-times–how-does-yours-rank.

26. www.humantransit.org/2014/09/reflections-on-world-commuting-times.html.

27. "Good Technology Survey Reveals Americans Are Working More, but on Their Own Schedule," *Good Technology Survey*, July 2, 2012.

28. The U.S. Department of Health and Human Services advises that adults do at least 150 minutes per week of moderate intensity physical activity, or 75 minutes per week of vigorous aerobic exercise.

29. Derek J. Roberts et al., "The 'Weekend Warrior': Fact or Fiction for Major Trauma?" *Canadian Journal of Surgery*, June 2014, 57(3): pp. E62–E68.

30. Rachel M. Henke, Ron Z. Goetzel, Janice McHugh, and Fik Isaac, "Recent Experience in Health Promotion at Johnson & Johnson: Lower Health Spending, Strong Return on Investment," *Health Affairs*, 2011, 30(3): pp. 490–499.

31. Katherine Baicker, David Cutler, and Zirui Song, "Workplace Wellness Programs Can Generate Savings," *Health Affairs*, February 2010, 29(2): pp. 304–311.

32. Raymond Fabius et al., "The Link Between Workforce Health and Safety and the Health of the Bottom Line: Tracking Market Performance of Companies That Nurture a 'Culture of Health,' " *American College of Occupational and Environmental Medicine*, September 2013, 55(9).

CHAPTER 2

1. If you can't make it to the exhibit, I recommend purchasing the companion book: Richard Potts and Christopher Sloan, *What Does It Mean to Be Human?*, National Geographic, March 9, 2010.

2. Modern humans, *Homo sapiens*, evolved from *Homo heidelbergensis* hominids, who evolved from *Homo erectus* hominids in Africa.

3. Richard Wrangham, "The Evolution of Human Nutrition," *Current Biology*, May 6, 2013, 23(9 R354).

4. W.R. Leonard, "The Global Diversity of Eating Patterns: Human Nutritional

Health in Comparative Perspective," *Physiol Behav*, 2014. dx.doi.org/10.1016/j.physbeh.2014.02.050.

5. Interview with Dr. Briana Pobiner of the Smithsonian Institution, July 10, 2014.

6. Marlene Zuk, *Paleofantasy: What Evolution Really Tells Us about Sex, Diet, and How We Live*, Norton, 2013.

7. Leonard, "The Global Diversity."

8. Ibid.

9. Richard Potts and Christopher Sloan, *What Does It Mean to be Human?* National Geographic, March 9, 2010, p. 150.

10. Ibid., p. 152.

11. Mira L. Katz et al., "Physical Activity Among Amish and Non-Amish Adults Living in Ohio Appalachia," *Journal of Community Health*, August 21, 2011, 37(2): pp. 434–440.

12. Steve Lohr, "Rethinking Privacy vs. Teamwork in Today's Workplace," *New York Times*, August 11, 1997.

13. Human factors and ergonomics are concerned with the application of what we know about people; their abilities, characteristics, and limitations; of the design of equipment they use; environments in which they function; and jobs they perform.

14. T.S. Church, D.M. Thomas, C. Tudor-Locke, P.T. Katzmarzyk, C.P. Earnest, et al., "Trends over 5 Decades in U.S. Occupation-Related Physical Activity and Their Associations with Obesity," *PLoS ONE*, 2011, 6(5): p. e19657.

15. HOK Global Workplace Statistics from 2011–2014.

16. Federal Reserve Economic Data (FRED) tool, Federal Reserve Bank of St. Louis, 2011 data, research.stlouisfed.org/fred2/.

17. "Good Technology Survey Reveals Americans Are Working More, but on Their Own Schedule," Good Technology Survey, July 2, 2012.

18. Right Management Survey, August 30, 2011. Available at www.right.com/news-and-events/press-releases/2011-press-releases/item21650.aspx.

19. Rose E. Oldham-Cooper, Charlotte A. Hardman, Charlotte E. Nicoll, Peter J. Rogers, and Jeffrey M. Brunstrom, "Playing a Computer Game During Lunch Affects Fullness, Memory for Lunch, and Later Snack Intake," *American Journal of Clinical Nutrition*, 2011, 93: pp. 308–313.

20. "Special Annual Report: Automatic Merchandiser State of the Vending Industry," vendingmarketwatch.com, June 2013.

21. Holly Ramer, "Health Law to Put Calorie Information on Vending Machines," Associated Press, December 28, 2013.

CHAPTER 3

1. www.worldbank.org/depweb/beyond/beyondco/beg_09.pdf.

2. Mihaly Csikszentmihalyi, *Flow: The Psychology of Optimal Experience*, Harper Perennial Modern Classics, 2008, pp. 48–67.

3. Steven Kotler, *The Rise of Superman: Decoding the Science of Ultimate Human Performance*, New Harvest, 2014.

4. Elizabeth Gaffney and Benjamin Ryder Howe, "David McCullough, The Art of Biography No. 2," *The Paris Review*, Fall 1999, 152.

5. Keith Sawyer, *Group Genius: The Creative Power of Collaboration*, Basic Books, 2008.

216

6. Want to know more about these units? Contact Diana D. Glawe, PhD, PE, LEED AP, Associate Professor, Engineering Science Department, Trinity University, or check out the units on digital commons: digitalcommons.trinity.edu/engine_faculty/8/.

7. Phone interview with David Ribble, September 16, 2015.

8. "IBM 2010 Global CEO Study: Creativity Selected as Most Crucial Factor for Future Success," May 18, 2010. www-935.ibm.com/services/us/en/c-suite/ceostudy2012/

9. Lauren Migliore, "The Aha! Moment: The Creative Science Behind Inspiration," *BrainWorld*, June 14, 2012.

10. Marily Oppezzo and Daniel L. Schwartz, "Give Your Ideas Some Legs: The Positive Effect of Walking on Creative Thinking," *Journal of Experimental Psychology: Learning, Memory, and Cognition*, 2014, 40(4): pp. 1142–1152.

11. Élise Labonté-LeMoyne et al., "The Delayed Effect of Treadmill Desk Usage on Recall and Attention," *Computers and Human Behavior*, May 2015, 46: pp. 1–5.

12. Jonah Lehrer, "How to Be Creative," *Wall Street Journal*, March 12, 2012.

13. Thomas Allen, "Architecture and Communication Among Product Development Engineers," *California Management Review*, 2007, 49(2), pp. 32–41.

14. Bruce Katz and Julie Wagner, "The Rise of Innovation Districts: A New Geography of Innovation in America," Metropolitan Policy Program, The Brookings Institution, May 2014.

15. Ibid.

16. Tores Theorell, "Working Conditions and Health," Chapter 5 in *Social Epidemiology*, edited by Lisa F. Berkman and Ichiro Kawachi, Oxford University Press, 2000.

17. Robert Karasek and Tores Theorell, *Healthy Work: Stress, Productivity, and the Reconstruction of Working Life*, Basic Books, 1990.

18. Confidential Global Workplace Survey, HOK, June 2015.

19. Sally Augustin, *Place Advantage: Applied Psychology for Interior Architecture*, Wiley, 2009.

20. Definitions from "Distributed Work Revisited Report," International Facility Management Association, September 2015.

21. Ibid., pp. 8–9. The following space descriptions may be unfamiliar to you. Touchdown spaces are designed for employees or visitors to work for a short period of time. Shared address space is an environment in which two or more employees share a single, assigned workspace, also referred to as desk sharing. Hoteling is an environment in which employees reserve workspace ahead of occupying it, and it accommodates situations where the facility has fewer workspaces than staff. Group address is a group or team space, designed to be used for a specified period. Free address space is shared on a first-come, first-served basis. These space types are not mutually exclusive. Often spaces can fall under more than one category.

22. Ibid., pp. 11.

CHAPTER 4

1. Catrine Tudor-Locke et al., "How Many Steps/day Are Enough? For Adults," *International Journal of Behavioral Nutrition and Physical Activity*, 2011, 8: p. 79.

2. Phone interview with Catrine Tudor-Locke, July 1, 2014.

3. Tudor-Locke et al., "How Many Steps/day."

4. Phone interview with Nate Costa, September 9, 2015.

5. Emily B. Kahn et al., "The Effectiveness of Interventions to Increase Physical Activity," *American Journal of Preventative Medicine*, 2002, p. 73.

6. Ibid., p. 77.

7. Flora Lichtman, "One Step to Combat Obesity: Make Stairs More Attractive," NPR.org, August 4, 2014.

8. C. Zimring et al., "Influences of Building Design and Site Design on Physical Activity: Research and Intervention Opportunities," *American Journal of Preventive Medicine*, 2005, 28(2S2): pp. 186–193; C.A.G. Boreham, W.F.M. Wallace, and A. Nevill, "Training Effects of Accumulated Daily Stair-Climbing Exercise in Previously Sedentary Young Women," *Preventive Medicine*, 2000, 30: pp. 277–281.

9. Maria Alvarez, " 'Active Design' for Affordable Housing," *Newsday*, July 31, 2013.

10. Peter Katzmarzyk, "Standing and Mortality in a Prospective Cohort of Canadian Adults," *American College of Sports* Medicine, 2014, 46(5): pp. 940-6

11. Markus Baer and Andrew P. Knight, "Get Up, Stand Up: The Effects of a Non-Sedentary Workspace on Information Elaboration and Group Performance," *Social Psychological and Personality Science*, June 12, 2014, 5: pp. 910-917

12. Andrew Tate, "Why Everyone From Beethoven, Goethe, Dickens, Darwin To Steve Jobs Took Long Walks and Why You Should Too," Canva blog, March 6, 2015.

13. P. Gordon-Larsen et al., "Inequality in the Built Environment Underlies Key Health Disparities in Physical Activity and Obesity," *Pediatrics*, 2006, 117(2): pp. 417–424.

14. R.E. Wener and G.W. Evans, "A Morning Stroll: Levels of Physical Activity in Car and Mass Transit Commuting," *Environment and Behavior*, 2007, 39: pp. 1–13.

15. T. Pikora, B. Giles-Corti, F. Bull, K. Jamrozik, and R. Donavan, "Developing a Framework for Assessment of the Environmental Determinants of Walking and Cycling," *Social Science and Medicine*, 2003, 56(8): pp. 1693–1704.

16. Agency for Healthcare Research and Quality, "The Effect of Health Care Working Conditions on Patient Safety." May 2003; Evidence Based Report/Technology Assessment, 2003 (74) AHRQ Publication 03-E024.

17. HOK Global Workplace Statistics from 2011–2014.

18. www.washingtonpost.com/business/economy/companies-take-a-broader-view-of-employee-wellness-programs/2015/06/08/e3b3f2c4-e1ed-11e4-81ea-0649268f729e_story.html.

19. Cliona Ni Mhurchu, Louise M. Aston, and Susan A. Jebb, "Effects of Worksite Health Promotion Interventions on Employee Diets: A Systematic Review," *BMC Public Health*, 2010, 10: p. 62.

20. The 2011 Living Social Dining Out Survey included 4,000 consumers in the top 20 U.S. media markets and was conducted by Mandala Research, LLC, 2011.

21. "People Management: The Google Way of Motivating Employees," *Entrepreneurial Insights Magazine*, September 25, 2014.

22. Brian Wansink, *Mindless Eating: Why We Eat More Than We Think*, Bantam, 2007.

23. J.S. Litt et al., "The Influence of Social Involvement, Neighborhood

Aesthetics, and Community Garden Participation on Fruit and Vegetable Consumption," *Am J Public Health*, 2011, 101(8): pp. 1466–1473.

24. Eskenazi Health press release, www.eskenazihealth.edu/Modules/News/8-19-13.

25. Phone interviews with Gale Tedhams of Owens Corning, June 1, 2015 and August 7, 2015.

CHAPTER 5

1. Quote from Sharon Salzberg during a panel at Wisdom 2.0 Business, New York, 2014.

2. www.webmd.com/balance/guide/causes-of-stress.

3. Sara Radicati and Quoc Hoan, *Email Statistics Report, 2011–2015*, The Radicati Group, Inc., May 2011, p. 3.

4. Sherry Turkle, *Alone Together: Why We Expect More from Technology and Less from Each Other*, Basic Books, 2012, p. 242.

5. Herbert Benson, *Relaxation Revolution: The Science and Genetics of Mind Body Healing*, Scribner, 2011, p. 56.

6. Dan Harris, *10% Happier: How I Tamed the Voice in My Head, Reduced Stress Without Losing My Edge, and Found Self-Help That Actually Works—A True Story*, It Books, 2014.

7. Steve Bradt, "Wandering Mind Not a Happy Mind," *Harvard Gazette*, November 11, 2010.

8. Britta K. Hölzel et al., "Mindfulness Practice Leads to Increases in Regional Brain Gray Matter Density," *Psychiatry Research: Neuroimaging*, January 2011, 191(1): pp. 36–43.

9. www.mayoclinic.org/tests-procedures/meditation/in-depth/meditation/art-20045858. Accessed August 17, 2015.

10. Phone interview with Joy Rains, September 2, 2014.

11. Ibid.

12. Phil You're listening to a sample of the Audible audio edition. Jackson, *Sacred Hoops: Spiritual Lessons of a Hardwood Warrior*, Hachette Books, 2006.

13. www.mindful.org/michael-gervais-mindfulness-and-high-performance-training-with-the-seahawks-video. Accessed August 17, 2015.

14. Douglas C. Johnson, "Modifying Resilience Mechanisms in At-Risk Individuals: A Controlled Study of Mindfulness Training in Marines Preparing for Deployment," *American Journal of Psychiatry*, August 2014, 171(8): pp. 844–853.

15. Jeffrey James, "How Steve Jobs Trained His Own Brain," *Inc. Magazine*, August 21, 2015.

16. Carol Harnett, "Mindfulness Comes to Work," *Human Resources Executive Magazine*, February 10, 2014.

17. David Gelles, "At Aetna, a C.E.O.'s Management by Mantra," *New York Times*, February 27, 2015.

18. beyondbodymindspirit.com/eileen-fisher-offers-free-wonderful-meditation-to-all#more-4705. Accessed August 17, 2015.

19. www.eileenfisher.com/EileenFisher/company/working_at_ef/Benefits_Wellness.jsp?bmLocale=en_US. Accessed August 17, 2015.

20. Study done by Russell Investment Group. www.greatplacetowork.com/our-approach/what-are-the-benefits-great-workplaces. Accessed August 21, 2015.

21. David Gelles, "The Mind Business," *Financial Times Magazine,* August 24, 2012.
22. Brad Wolfe, "Five Tips for Launching a Meditation Program at Work," *Greater Good,* June 8, 2015.
23. Peter Bregman, "How (and Why) to Stop Multitasking," *Harvard Business Review,* May 20, 2010.

24. Phone interview with Sam Sidhu, July 24, 2015.
25. Franklin Becker, "Organizational Ecology and Knowledge Networks," *California Management Review,* 2007, 49(2): pp. 42–61.
26. "State of the American Workplace: Employee Engagement Insights for U.S. Business," *Leaders,* Gallup, 2013, p. 29.
27. International Facility Management Association, "Distributed Work Revisited Report," September 2015, p. 31.
28. Quentin Fottrell, "Americans Only Take Half of Their Paid Vacation," *MarketWatch,* October 31, 2014.
29. David Weinburg, "Americans Not Taking Vacation, and It Hurts," *Marketplace,* November 27, 2012.
30. share.kaiserpermanente.org/article/kaiser-permanente-expands-colorado-youth-programming-through-new-arts-integrated-resources/.
31. www.news.vcu.edu/article/Benefits_of_Taking_Fido_to_Work_May_Not_Be_Far_Fetched.
32. Melissa Hincha-Ownby, "10 Companies That Let You Bring Your Dog to Work," *Mother Nature Network,* August 19, 2011.

CHAPTER 6

1. Brett Smith, "Sleep Deprivation Is A Global Epidemic, Says International Sleep Study," *Red Orbit,* September 3, 2013.
2. www.cdc.gov/sleep/.
3. Bronwyn Fryer, "Sleep Deficit: The Performance Killer," *Harvard Business Review,* October 2006.
4. Sangheon Lee, Deirdre McCann, and Jon C. Messenger, "Working Time Around the World," *International Labour Organization,* 2007.
5. sleepfoundation.org/sleep-topics/women-and-sleep/.
6. Mark R. Rosekind et al., "The Cost of Poor Sleep: Workplace Productivity Loss and Associated Costs," *Journal of Occupational and Environmental Medicine,* January 2010, 52(1): pp. 91–98.
7. Tom Rath and James K. Harter, *Well-Being: The Five Essential Elements,* Gallup Press, 2010.
8. www.webmd.com/sleep-disorders/guide/sleep-101.
9. Amie M. Gordon, "Your Sleep Cycle Revealed," *Psychology Today,* July 26, 2013.
10. Ut Na Sio, Padraic Monaghan and Tom Ormerod, "Sleep on It, but Only If It Is Difficult: Effects of Sleep on Problem Solving," *Memory & Cognition,* February 2013, 41(2): pp. 159–166.
11. Ullrich Wagner, Steffen Gais, Hilde Haider, Rolf Verleger & Jan Born," Sleep inspires insight," *Nature,* January 2004, 427:pp. 352–355.; Received 21 August 2003; Accepted 17 November 2003.
12. www.thefiscaltimes.com/Articles/2012/07/23/Sleepless-in-America-A-32-4-Billion-Business.

13. www.npr.org/sections/thesalt/2012/05/15/152690836/jetlagged-by-your-social-calendar-better-check-your-waistline.

14. "How the Cycles of Light and Darkness Affect Your Health and Well-Being," Joseph Mercola interview with Dan Pardi, Mercola.com, January 19, 2014.

15. Pat Hagan, "Work in an Office with No Windows? It Could Cost You 46 Minutes of Sleep a Night," *Daily Mail*, August 2014.

16. The team of people working on this system with David Conrath included a forward-thinking faculty team; architect Doug Gehley, who heads the facilities committee at Bishop O'Connell; former NASA photobiologist Robert Soler; Dr. Luis Eljaiek, chief medical officer for Anthrospheres; and Dr. Susan Macey, chief wellness officer for Anthrospheres.

17. Interview and tour with David Conrath at Bishop O'Connell High School, Falls Church, Virginia, September 18, 2015.

18. C.S. Pechacek, M. Andersen, and S. W. Lockley, "Preliminary Method for Prospective Analysis of the Circadian Efficacy of Daylight with Applications to Healthcare Architecture," *Leukos*, 2008, 5(1): pp. 1–26.

19. Interview and tour with David Conrath.

20. J. Veitch, G. Newsham, P. Boyce, and C. Jones, "Lighting Appraisal, Well-Being and Performance in Open-Plan Offices: A Linked Mechanisms Approach," *Lighting Research and Technology*, 2008, 40(2): pp. 133–151.

21. Brittany Wood, Mark S. Rea, Barbara Plitnick, and Mariana G. Figuerio, "Light Level and Duration of Exposure Determine the Impact of Self-Luminous Tablets on Melatonin Suppression," *Applied Ergonomics*, March 2013, 44(2): pp. 237–240.

22. "How the Cycles of Light and Darkness."

23. Tim Ferris podcast, "The Oracle of Silicon Valley, Reid Hoffman (Plus: Michael McCullough)," fourhourworkweek.com/2015/08/31/the-oracle-of-silicon-valley-reid-hoffman-plus-michael-mccullough/.

24. sleepfoundation.org/sleep-topics/shift-work-and-sleep.

25. A number of laboratory and field studies have shown that light exposure at night attenuates subjective and objective indices of sleepiness, while improving alertness and performance. Most of these studies used bright light of greater than 1,000 lux, but the alerting effects of light may be present at room light levels of only 100–200 lux in subjects who have been adapted to dim light. The WELL Building Standard suggests that at least 75 percent of work points should have at least 250 melanopic lux for at least four hours per day for every day of the year for "typical" work environments (not specifying shift work).

26. Arianna Huffington gives a more detailed account of her scary health episode in the introduction to her book *Thrive: The Third Metric to Redefining Success and Creating a Life of Well-Being, Wisdom, and Wonder* (Harmony, 2014). Her tips on sleep in this book are excellent.

CHAPTER 7

1. Bruce Bridgeman, *Psychology and Evolution: The Origins of Mind*, SAGE Publications, 2003, pp. 61–62.

2. Stephen R. Kellert, Judith H. Heerwagen, and Martin L. Mador, *Biophilic Design: The Theory, Science, and Practice of Bringing Buildings to Life*, Wiley, 2008, p 23.

3. Ibid, p 228.

4. O. Kardan et al., "Neighborhood Greenspace and Health in a Large Urban Center," *Sci. Rep.*, 2015, 5: p. 11610.

5. *The Economics of Biophilia*, Terrapin Bright Green, LLC, 2012, p. 9.

6. R. Cooper, "The Psychology of Boredom," *Science Journal*, 1968, 4(2): pp. 38–42.

7. Judith H. Heerwagen, "Investing In People: The Social Benefits of Sustainable Design," Working Paper, Rethinking Sustainable Construction 2006 Conference, Sarasota, Florida, September 2006. Available at 74.125.93.104/ search?q=cache:xScIqta2SOwJ:courses.caup.washington.edu/ARCH/498G/ JHInvestinginPeople.

8. Cooper, "Psychology of Boredom."

9. L. Heschong, "Windows and Office Worker Performance: The SMUD Call Center and Desktop Studies," in *Creating the Productive Workplace*, second edition, edited by D. Clements-Croome, Taylor & Francis, 2006, pp. 277–309.

10. I. Elzeyadi, "Daylighting-Bias and Biophilia: Quantifying the Impact of Daylight on Occupants' Health," Greenbuild 2011 Proceedings, USGBC Press, 2011.

11. R.S. Ulrich, "View Through a Window May Influence Recovery from Surgery," *Science*, 1984, 224.

12. Lisa Heschong, Roger L. Wright, and Stacia Okura, "Daylighting Impacts on Human Performance in School," *Journal of the Illuminating Engineering Society*, Summer 2002.

13. F. Becker and F. Steele, *Workplace by Design*, Jossey-Bass, 1995.

14. A. Kjellberg, U. Landstrom, M. Tesarz, L. Soderberg, and E. Akerlund, "The Effects Of Nonphysical Noise Characteristics, Ongoing Task and Noise Sensitivity on Annoyance and Distraction Due to Noise at Work," *Journal of Environmental Psychology*, 1996, 16: pp.123–136.

15. F.R.H. Zijlstra, R.A. Roe, A.B. Leonora, and I. Krediet, "Temporal Factors in Mental Work: Effects of Interrupted Activities," *Journal of Occupational and Organizational Psychology*, 1999, 72: pp. 163–185.

16. *Sound Matters: How to Achieve Acoustic Comfort in the Contemporary Office*, U.S. General Services Administration, GSA Public Buildings Service, December 2011.

17. Sally Augustin, *Place Advantage: Applied Psychology for Interior Architecture*, Wiley, 2009.

18. Ibid.

19. Alpa V. Patel, Leslie Bernstein, Anusila Deka, Heather Spencer Feigelson, Peter T. Campbell, Susan M. Gapstur, Graham A. Colditz, and Michael J. Thun. "Leisure Time Spent Sitting in Relation to Total Mortality in a Prospective Cohort of US Adults," *Am J Epid*, published online July 22, 2010 (doi: 10.1093/ aje/kwq155).

20. *Clearing the Air: Asthma and Indoor Air Exposures*, Committee on the Assessment of Asthma and Indoor Air, Division of Health Promotion and Disease Prevention, Institute of Medicine, National Academy of Sciences, 2000.

21. Sick building syndrome is a combination of ailments associated with an individual's place of work or residence. Sick building causes are frequently pinned down to flaws in the heating, ventilation, and air conditioning (HVAC) systems. Other causes have been attributed to contaminants produced by

outgassing of some types of building materials, volatile organic compounds, molds, improper exhaust ventilation of light industrial chemicals used within, or fresh-air intake location/lack of adequate air filtration.

22. G. Kats, L. Alevantis, A. Berman, E. Mills, and J. Perlman, "The Costs and Financial Benefits of Green Buildings: A Report to California's Sustainable Building Taskforce," October 2003.

23. S. Tanabe, N. Nishihara, and M. Haneda, "Indoor Temperature, Productivity, and Fatigue in Office Tasks," *HVAC&R Research*, 2007, 13(4): pp. 623–633.

24. T. Witterseh, D. Wyon, and G. Clausen, "The Effects of Moderate Heat Stress and Open-Plan Office Noise Distraction on SBS Symptoms and on the Performance of Office Work," *Indoor Air*, 2004, 14 (Suppl. 8): pp. 30–40.

25. W. Kroner, J.A. Stark-Martin, and T. Willemain, "Using Advanced Office Technology to Increase Productivity," Working Paper, Rensselaer Polytechnic Institute, Center for Architectural Research, 1992.

26. www.aaos.org/news/aaosnow/dec08/clinical10.asp.

27. "Nonfatal Occupational Injuries and Illnesses Requiring Days Away from Work, 2012," U.S. Bureau of Labor Statistics, November 26, 2013.

28. Christine Sprigg, Christopher Stride, Toby Wall, David Holman, and Phoebe Smith, "Work Characteristics, Musculoskeletal Disorders, and the Mediating Role of Psychological Strain: A Study of Call Center Employees," *Journal of Applied Psychology*, 2008, 92(5): pp. 1456–1466.

29. Leigh Stringer, "Using Facebook to Transform the Workplace," HOK White Paper, 2013.

30. Erik Peper and I-Mei Lin, "Increase or Decrease Depression: How Body Postures Influence Your Energy Level," *Biofeedback*, Fall 2012, 40(3): pp. 125–130.

31. centerforactivedesign.org.

32. delosliving.com.

33. Melissa Walker, "Healthy Design, Healthy Building, Healthy City" workshop, American Institute of Architects District Architecture Center, August 25, 2015.

34. Joan Meyers-Levy and Rui (Juliet) Zhu, "The Influence of Ceiling Height: The Effect of Priming on the Type of Processing That People Use," *Journal of Consumer Research*, August 2007, 34(2): pp. 174–186.

35. C. Cooper-Marcus and M. Barnes, editors, *Healing Gardens: Therapeutic Benefits and Design Recommendations*, Wiley, 1999.

36. S. Kaplan, J. Talbot, and R. Kaplan, "Coping with Daily Hassles: The Impact of Nearby Nature on the Work Environment," Project Report, U.S. Forest Service, North Central Forest Experience Stations, Urban Forestry Unit Cooperative Agreement 23-85-08, U.S. Government Printing Office, 1988.

37. F.L. Olmsted, F.L., *The Value and Care of Parks*, Report to the Congress of the State of California, 1865.

38. Susanne Gargiulo, "Can a Humble Houseplant Make You More Creative?" CNN, October 31, 2014.

39. David Fell, "Wood in the Human Environment: Restorative Properties of Wood in the Built Interior Environment," dissertation, University of British Columbia, 2010.

40. Kathleen D. Vohs, Joseph P. Redden, and Ryan Rahinel, "Tidy Desk or Messy Desk? Each Has Its Benefits," *Science Daily*, August 6, 2013.

41. Neville Owen, Genevieve N. Healy, Charles E. Matthews, and David W. Dunstan, "Too Much Sitting: The Population Health Science of Sedentary Behavior," *Exercise and Sport Sciences Reviews*, 2010.

42. "Sound Matters."

43. N. Kwallek, K. Soon, and C.M. Lewis, "Work Week Productivity, Visual Complexity, and Individual Environmental Sensitivity in Three Offices of Different Color Interiors," *Color Research and Application*, 2006, 32(2): pp. 130–143.

44. Stephanie Lichtenfeld, Andrew J. Elliot, Markus A. Maier, and Reinhard Pekrun, "Fertile Green: Green Facilitates Creative Performance," *Personality and Social Psychology Bulletin*, 2012, 38(6): pp. 784–797.

45. Ashley Welsh, "How Fast Can a Virus Spread? Faster Than You Think," *Everyday Health*, September 8, 2014.

46. Christina Bodin Danielsson, "Office Type in Relation to Health, Well-Being, and Job Satisfaction Among Employees," *Environment & Behavior*, September 2009, 40(5): pp. 636–668.

47. Jon Card, "Tips for Boosting Productivity with Good Office Design," *The Guardian*, January 23, 2014.

48. Ann McKim and Jo Ellyn Pederson, "Step into My Office: The Effects of Organization and Lemon Scent on Mood," presentation at the 2011 Annual Meeting of the American Psychological Association, Washington, DC.

CHAPTER 8

1. T.E. Deal and A.A. Kennedy, *Corporate Cultures: The Rites and Rituals of Corporate Life*, Penguin Books, 1982; Perseus Books reissue, 2000.

2. Jodi Kantor and David Streitfeld, "Inside Amazon: Wrestling Big Ideas in a Bruising Workplace," *New York Times*, August 15, 2015.

3. The Robert Wood Johnson Foundation's website describes a culture of health. As stated by Risa Lavizzo-Mourey, the president and CEO, "It calls for us, as a nation, to strive together to build a Culture of Health enabling all in our diverse society to lead healthier lives, now and for generations to come."

4. Interview with Sarah Kalamchi and Peter Chiarchiaro at Next Jump, July 9, 2015.

5. Ed O'Boyle and Jim Harter, "Why Your Workplace Wellness Program Isn't Working," *Gallup Business Journal*, May 13, 2014.

6. Interview with Sam Whiteside and several employees at The Motley Fool, August 21, 2015.

7. "Wearables at Work: A Technical Brief," The Vitality Group, April 2014.

8. Brian Shilling, "What Happened When GE Paid Employees to Quit Smoking?" The Commonwealth Fund, June 16, 2009.

9. www.path.org/about/microsoft.

10. "The New Health Care Imperative: Driving Performance, Connecting to Value," 19th Annual Towers Watson/National Business Group on Health Employer Survey on Purchasing Value in Health Care, Towers Watson, May 2014, p. 20.

11. Julie Appleby, "When Does Workplace Wellness Become Coercive?" NPR. org, June 24, 2015.

12. A.V. Carron, H.A. Hausenblas, and D. Mack, "Social Influence and Exercise: A Meta-Analysis," *Journal of Sport & Exercise Psychology*, 1996, 18(1): pp. 1–16.

13. Phone interview with Tim Church, July 24, 2014.

14. Phone interview with Mike Tinney, September 10, 2014.

15. "A Randomized Controlled Trial: The Effects of SuperBetter on Depression," University of Pennsylvania in collaboration with SuperBetter Labs, LLC, July 15, 2013.

16. Jessica Skorka-Brown, Jackie Andrade, Ben Whalley, and Jon May, "Playing Tetris Decreases Drug and Other Cravings in Real World Settings," *Addictive Behaviors*, December 2015, 51: pp. 165–170.

17. Tim Ferris podcast, "Jane McGonigal on Getting More Done with Less Stress and The Health Benefits of Gaming," fourhourworkweek.com/2015/07/28/jane-mcgonigal/.

18. "The New Health Care Imperative."

19. Quote from Golbie Kamarei during a panel at Wisdom 2.0 Business, New York, 2014.

CHAPTER 9

1. Phone interviews with Gale Tedhams, June 1, 2015 and August 7, 2015.

2. Michael E. Porter and Mark R. Kramer, "Creating Shared Value," *Harvard Business Review*, January-February 2011.

3. Robert G. Eccles, Ioannis Ioannou, and George Serafeim, "The Impact of Corporate Sustainability on Organizational Processes and Performance," National Bureau of Economic Research, Working Paper 17950, March 2012, p. 25.

4. Vera Oziransky, Derek Yach, Tsu-Yu Tsao, Alexandra Luterek, and Denise Stevens, "Beyond the Four Walls: Why the Community Is Critical to Workforce Health," Vitality Institute, July 2015, p. II.

5. Edelman Goodpurpose® 2012 Global Consumer Survey. Available at http://www.fairtrade.travel/uploads/files/Edelman_Goodpurpose_-_Global_Consumer_Survey.pdf. Accessed August 5, 2015.

6. assets.wholefoodsmarket.com/www/company-info/investor-relations/annual-reports/2014-WFM-AR-Stakeholder-Letter.pdf.

7. www.hsph.harvard.edu/sensorsforhealth/health-performance-indicators/.

8. David Blumenthal, Elizabeth Malphrus, and J. Michael McGinnis, editors, "Vital Signs: Core Metrics for Health and Health Care Progress," Committee on Core Metrics for Better Health at Lower Cost, Institute of Medicine, 2015, p. S-5.

9. Katherine Baicker, David Cutler, and Zirui Song, "Workplace Wellness Programs Can Generate Savings," *Health Affairs*, February 2010, 29(2): pp. 304–311.

10. Rachel M. Henke, Ron Z. Goetzel, Janice McHugh, and Fik Isaac, "Recent Experience in Health Promotion at Johnson & Johnson: Lower Health Spending, Strong Return on Investment," *Health Affairs*, 2011, 30(3): pp. 490–499; B.L. Naydek, J.A. Pearson, R.J. Ozminkowski, B.T. Day, and R.Z. Goetzel, "The Impact of the Highmark Employee Wellness Programs on 4-Year Healthcare Costs," *Occupational Environmental Medicine*, February 2008, 50(2): pp. 146–156; R.J. Ozminkowski, R.L. Dunn, R.Z. Goetzel, R.I. Cantor, J. Murnane, and M. Harrison, "A Return on Investment Evaluation of the Citibank, N.A., Health Management Program," *Am J Health Promot*, 1999, 14(1): pp. 31–43.

11. I. Elzeyadi, "Daylighting-Bias and Biophilia: Quantifying the Impact of Daylight on Occupants' Health," Greenbuild 2011 Proceedings, USGBC Press,

2011; R.S. Ulrich, "View Through a Window May Influence Recovery from Surgery," *Science*, 1984, 224.

12. Robert J. Laverne and Kimberly Winson-Geideman, "The Influence of Trees and Landscaping on Rental Rates at Office Buildings," *Journal of Arboriculture*, September 2003, 29(5).

13. Matthew Strozier, "The Cost of a View, A New Price Breakdown Shows How Much Co-op and Condo Owner Pay by Floor," *The Real Deal*, June 1, 2010.

14. Anita Kramer, Terry Lassar, Mark Federman, and Sara Hammerschmidt, "Building for Wellness: The Business Case," Urban Land Institute, 2014.

15. www.shrm.org/hrdisciplines/benefits/articles/pages/wellness_employeeretention.aspx#sthash.UV95YcZF.dpuf.

16. http://www.payscale.com/data-packages/employee-loyalty/full-list.

17. Christina Farr, "Silicon Valley Takes Benefits 'Arms Race' to Health Care," Reuters, October 2, 2014.

18. Raymond Fabius et al., "The Link Between Workforce Health and Safety and the Health of the Bottom Line: Tracking Market Performance of Companies That Nurture a 'Culture of Health,'" *American College of Occupational and Environmental Medicine*, September 2013, 55(9).

19. James Harter et al., "Causal Impact of Employee Work Perceptions on the Bottom Line of Organizations," *Association for Psychological Science*, 2010, p. 387.

20. www.chaa.org/winners/2013/Summary%20Report%20-%20CHAA%20Amex%202013.pdf.

21. www.chaa.org/winners/2012/Smithsonian%20Final%20Summary%20Report.pdf.

22. T.S. Church, D.M. Thomas, C. Tudor-Locke, P.T. Katzmarzyk, C.P. Earnest, et al., "Trends over 5 Decades in U.S. Occupation-Related Physical Activity and Their Associations with Obesity," *PLoS ONE*, 2011, 6(5): p. e19657.

23. "The Quick Grab: Top Snacks in Dollar Sales from Vending Machines, According to Automatic Merchandiser," *Washington Post*, May 19, 2008.

24. www.niddk.nih.gov/health-information/health-statistics/Pages/overweight-obesity-statistics.aspx.

25. Arthur C. Nelson, "Toward a New Metropolis: The Opportunity to Rebuild America," Virginia Polytechnic Institute and State University, Discussion Paper Prepared for The Brookings Institution Metropolitan Policy Program, December 2004.

26. Bruce Katz and Julie Wagner, "The Rise of Innovation Districts: A New Geography of Innovation in America," Metropolitan Policy Program, The Brookings Institution, May 2014.

27. "The Changing Nature of Consumer Health," Accenture White Paper, 2014. Available at www.accenture.com/us-en/insight-consumer-healthcare-market-high-performance-business-research-2013.aspx.

28. Think this is a little too futuristic? Check out the competition submission for an "algae clad" net-zero retrofit of an existing Los Angeles federal office building in *Metropolis Magazine* led by young designers and engineers from HOK and Vanderweil: www.metropolismag.com/May-2011/Group-Effort-The-Next-Generation-2011-Winner/.

ABOUT THE AUTHOR

LEIGH STRINGER IS A LEADERSHIP in Energy & Environmental Design Accredited Professional (LEED AP), workplace strategy expert, and researcher whose work has been covered by national media, including CNN, *USA Today*, the *Wall Street Journal*, and *Good Morning America*. She works for EYP, an architecture, engineering, and building technology firm. She is the author of the best-selling book *The Green Workplace: Sustainable Strategies that Benefit Employees, the Environment and the Bottom Line*, a guide to green business practices that benefit employees while enhancing business profitability and long-term marketability.

Leigh works with corporate, government, higher education, and institutional clients to help them create sustainable and high-performing workplace environments that enhance well-being and human performance. She has worked with, among others, Google, Cisco Systems, Under Armour, LG, Johnson & Johnson, GlaxoSmithKline, Bank of America, Zurich Financial, Ernst & Young, American Express, The MITRE Corporation, the Architect of the U.S. Capitol, the British House of Commons, the U.S. General Services Administration, the World Wildlife Fund, the Carnegie Corporation of New York, Baylor University, Washington University in St. Louis, and Heathrow Airport.

Leigh is currently collaborating with Harvard University's School of Public Health, the Center for Active Design in New York, the International Facility Management Association, and the AIA DC Chapter on Health and Well-Being to create new tools to connect like minds and to blur the boundaries across industries in order to advance and improve our well-being at work. She regularly speaks at the U.S. Green Building Council, CoreNet Global, the International Facility Management Association, and the American Institute of Architects events and writes for a number of workplace and real estate magazines and journals, along with her blog, LeighStringer.com.

Leigh has a Bachelor of Arts, a Masters of Architecture, and an MBA from Washington University in St. Louis. She lives with her husband and two daughters in Washington, DC.